Classics In
Child Development

Classics In
Child Development

GENIUS AND STUPIDITY

Lewis M. Terman

ARNO PRESS

A New York Times Company

New York — 1975

Reprint Edition 1975 by Arno Press Inc.

Classics in Child Development
ISBN for complete set: 0-405-06450-0
See last pages of this volume for titles.

Manufactured in the United States of America

Library of Congress Cataloging in Publication Data

Terman, Lewis Madison, 1877-1956.
  Genius and stupidity.

  (Classics in child development)
  Reprint of the 1906 ed., which was originally pre-
sented as the author's thesis, Clark University.
  1. Intellect. 2. Genius. 3. Inefficiency,
Intellectual. I. Title. II. Series.
BF431.T39 1975   153.9   74-21430
ISBN 0-405-06479-9

GENIUS AND STUPIDITY.

A Study of some of the Intellectual Processes of Seven "Bright" and Seven "Stupid" Boys.

By Lewis M. Terman,
Sometime Fellow in Psychology, Clark University.

CONTENTS.

I.   Introduction: Psychology and Life.

One of the most serious problems confronting psychology is that of connecting itself with life. The wholly modern development of psychiatry and criminology, the recent activities in individual psychology, a continuous tempest of articles, pamphlets, and books on the relations of psychology to education, all point to the fundamental importance of the task.

This problem offers itself not to psychology alone but to all the sciences, and it may be said that they have excuse for existence only to the extent to which they are capable of framing a solution. Humanity has a vested right to demand of the scientist now and then that he show his hand. Theory that does not some way affect life has no value. Morever, as President William Lowe Bryan has pointed out, (3) such theory is *ipso facto* not true. That it seems so is due to the "illusion of precision," in the interest of which we shut out from consideration all of reality except the portion immediately before us. Why wonder, then, that that atom has no connection with the manifold from which we took it?

It hardly need be said that other sciences have bridged this chasm more successfully than psychology. In the words of Spearman, "When we pass an electric current through water until it vaporizes into bubbles of hydrogen and oxygen, we can be tolerably certain that we have still got in our jars almost the whole of the same material substance, only reduced to simple form. But when we assert that the decision of Regulus to vote against making peace with Carthage was no more than a conglomeration of visual, auditory and tactual sensations in various stages of intensity and association, then there is an undeniable risk that some precious psychical elements may have slipped through our fingers." (18, p. 204.)

On the other hand, John Stuart Mill held that the common opinion that the thought, sentiments, and actions of human beings cannot be the object of science, rests upon the confounding of all science with exact science. Mill conceived an intermediate between the perfection of science and its extreme imperfection. For example, a phenomenon may result from two sorts of causes; from major causes accessible to observation and calculation, and from minor, secondary causes not thus accessible. In such a case we shall be able to account for the principal part of the phenomenon, but there will be variations and modifications which we cannot completely explain. Mill compares the science of human nature with the science of the tides, which can never become exact in the strict sense, and yet is exact enough to be practically useful. The exactness is not like that of present astronomy, but more comparable to the condition of astronomy when its calculations included only the principal facts and not the perturbations. Ribot, speaking of Mill's proposed science of *Ethology*, says: "No doubt this science will always partake considerably of the nature of art; will it not be sufficiently exact, however, to render its employment legitimate? The naturalists have discovered certain organic correlations on which they rely for the reconstruction of an animal from a few fragments. Might not the psychological conditions be equally arrived at? Let us suppose that by an accumulation of sure and varied experiments we were enabled to establish, for instance, that a certain manner of feeling supposes a certain variety of imagination, which in its turn supposes a certain mode of judgment and reasoning, which again supposes a certain method of acting; and let us suppose that this determination should be as precise as possible. Then by the aid of a few facts it might be possible to reconstruct a character, since the problem would reduce itself to the following: Given a member of the series to find the entire series."

The sciences, as Comte observed, were historically produced in the order of decreasing generality. We need, therefore, no greater proof of the lingering of psychology in its infancy than the striking fact that little application has proceeded from it.

Thus it was for centuries with physics and chemistry, thus also with the biological sciences, whose results are yet only dimly foreseen. The difference among the sciences in this respect lies partly in the subject matter; whether it is living or inert. But the difficulty is not thus wholly accounted for. The biologist is not nearly so badly off as the psychologist. He knows a particular plant or animal organism better than any ordinary individual does, while on the other hand it has passed into proverb that of all men the psychologist is the most helpless before the individual mind. If taken to task, he pleads the doubtful excuse that it is his business to know mind in general and that he has nothing to do with this or that individual mind. Can we wonder that the mathematician, physicist, or even the biologist, who, like the psychologist, deals with life, should smile occasionally at the artificial constructions of psychology?

One thing seems certain; viz., that psychology and life cannot be connected until we have transcended the psychology of structure. To that end psychology will need to follow in the path of biology, which is becoming increasingly dynamic. From this point of view, the *structure* of the animal or plant does not concern us except as it shapes the force of the organism as a dynamic agency. It is thus that the chasm between the old morphology and life is being spanned. If psychology would seriously enlarge its *raison d'être* it must follow this example.

On the other hand, it is asserted, as by Professor Titchener (22), that whatever may be in store for a future functional psychology, the present demand is more pressing for the study of structural elements. It is true that always in the history of science, the static and structural aspects receive attention first, just as in biology anatomy developed before physiology. But in psychology there is already a tendency in the opposite direction. We are beginning to realize that the hypostasized segment of consciousness known as sensation is not the ultimate and true reality. In psychology, function, in part at least, produces structure. We cannot truly know what consciousness is, till we know what it does. Professor James has succeeded in giving meaning to our conscious states without breaking them up into fragments. "On the whole," he says (8), "I venture still to think that we really gain a more living understanding of the mind by keeping our attention as long as possible upon our entire conscious states as they are concretely given to us, than by a post mortem study of their comminuted 'elements.' This last is the study of artificial abstractions, not of natural things." This conception, if logically carried out, can only end by extending the field of psychology to include logic, ethics, and æsthetics. Logic becomes the applied psychology of reasoning, ethics the psychology of motives and impulses, and æsthetics a chapter in the psychology of the emotions.

The earliest attempt, at least in modern times, at a direct relating of psychology and life, was phrenology. This, science at once disowned. More recently the French have made, on little larger empirical basis, elaborate classifications of types of character. Over against these we have the empirical work coming under the head of *mental tests*. This latter work is of two sorts: one embracing a small amount of data from each of a vast number of individuals, and the other made up of intensive studies of a very few subjects. A large number of such intensive studies would seem to offer a better basis than can be gained in any other way for a psychology of character or temperament, or for any scientific classifications from the psychological point of view.

But at the outset it may be objected that the differentiæ which mark off types of mentality from each other are not proper subject matter for psychology, that they touch us only on the practical side, and that if we would seek justice to the great synthesis of reality we must look to art. In freely awarding this function to art, as is obviously its due, we do not thereby invalidate the claims of individual psychology. All individual differences of fundamental importance are subject matter for general psychology. Comparative psychology deals with the largest of these differences. Age and sex differences already receive careful attention from most workers. It is only the minor differences—those unessential to science—that psychology is willing to surrender to the domain of art. The contention here made is that over and above these minor differences there are deep and fundamental lines of cleavage among individual mentalities the existence of which is as yet hardly suspected; that in dealing with individual minds we encounter no smaller differences than the zoölogist finds in his own field.

But we have only to compare the relative status of the zoölogist and psychologist to see how the latter has lagged behind. While the zoölogist has no longer any difficulty in stating the essential differences between even such superficially similar animals as the whale and the fish, psychologists cannot agree on the features distinguishing the most widely separated grades of intelligence. And yet there is certainly as much variety in psychical types as in the physical. One important difference is that the psychologist has to deal with facts more hidden from direct observation. The differences, however, when found, are certainly as great in one case as in the other.

This advocacy of a scientific classification does not mean to cast discredit upon the practical classifications that grow out of every-day experience. Far from discrediting classifications that have been found serviceable, the kind of work here advocated, would simply follow the example of Linnæus in seeking for more fundamental bases of division.

Such study, moreover, cannot fail to be rich in pedagogical suggestions. Just as the laboratory study of comparative psychology has justified itself both by its suggestiveness for general psychology and for education, as well as from the standpoint of evolutionary theory, so should experimental results gradually replace the "interesting stories" about children. Along the line of mental tests, a few psychologists entertain serious expectations of immediate practical results. Binet, for example, in 1896 expressed the hope that he would soon succeed in devising a series of mental and motor tests which would be so simple that even the ordinary parent could apply them to his child and in an hour or two reach results which would indicate definitely the child's grade of intelligence. Others have recommended such tests as helps for the physician. Simon (17) states, regarding the method of the "copy," "convenient, short, and exact, this copying of phrases constitutes a good method of diagnosing a child's intellectual development at the very moment of the experiment. Kirkpatrick (10) thinks his tests should be of some value to the school superintendent or teacher in settling doubtful cases of promotion. Bolton (2), speaking of the unsatisfactoriness of the ordinary school examination and of the need of replacing it by something more scientific, suggests that "Tests of physical endowment and of general healthiness of body seem to offer the most promise of finding what is wanted." It is implied, also, that in other walks of life such tests will come in to determine fitness to do various kinds of work. Galton long ago remarked that "One of the most important objects of measurement . . . is to obtain a general knowledge of the capacities of a man by sinking shafts, as it were, at a few critical points." Near the close of one of the most important contributions yet made to the subject, namely, that by Spearman (18, p. 277), we have the following statement: "Here would seem to be the long wanted general rational basis for public examinations. Instead of continuing ineffectively to protest that high marks in Greek Syntax are no test as to the capacity of men to command troops or to administer provinces, we shall at last actually determine the precise accuracy of the various means of measuring General Intelligence, and then we shall in an equally positive manner ascertain the exact relative importance of this General Intelligence as compared with the other characteristics desirable for the particular post which the candidate is to assume. Thus it is hoped we shall eventually reach our pedagogical conclusions, not by easy subjective theories, nor by the insignificant range of personal experience, nor yet by some catchpenny exceptional cases, but rather by an adequately representative array of established facts.''

It must be admitted that expectations along the line of the above suggestions are little justified by the results already obtained by such tests. The requirements of the psychological laboratory can no more be simplified so as to be met by the ordinary parent or teacher than can those of the physical or biological laboratory. In the light of present conditions, the suggestion recently made by Cattell (4) seems much more reasonable; namely, that there is destined to grow up eventually a large body of psychological experts who will play a rôle in the future as important as that of the medical men at present. The.wide and varied usefulness of such a body, supposing them to exist and to be adequately equipped, need not be insisted upon. Psychology can, however, do more harm than good in the educational field and in its other fields of possible usefulness if its results are prematurely applied.

We need not argue the point further. The following study, at least, is undertaken in the faith that psychology and life are not prime to each other, and that even at present some of the common factors may be sought without thereby cheapening either the methods or results of experimental psychology. How extremely little is herein contributed to this end, no one is better aware of than the writer; but he would fain co-operate with the pioneers already at work, and ventures to offer the following account of his experiments for what it may contribute to the choice and evaluation of methods in this comparatively new field.

II. NATURE, PURPOSE, AND CONDITIONS OF THE STUDY.

Studies with mental tests readily fall into two chief classes. On the one hand, (A) are the more or less superficial tests of a large number of individuals. These again are of two sorts: (1) Those which, in sets perhaps of ten to twenty tests, hope to mark off in the space of an hour or two the chief facts in one's whole mental individuality. These are usually made, as has been said, with a large number of subjects and therefore are liable to be hurriedly and roughly executed, and often with the help of half-trained assistants. (2) Such work as that of Spearman, already referred to, which also uses a large number of subjects, but instead of trying to mark off the entire personality aims at testing one or a few traits under very carefully controlled conditions. But all tests of the A group aim at exact quantitative results.   They are psychophysical.   They must be so planned that they will not allow of several different types of reaction, but so that the results shall present only units of *quantitative* difference.   The aim is mathematical correlation, and the individual subject has no place in the interpretation of results.

There is another approach, (B) quite different from the above, aiming more at a *qualitative* analysis of the processes involved.   Examples are the work of Kraepelin and his students in Germany, Binet in France, and Sharp and Kuhlmann in America.   This method prefers a few subjects carefully studied. It aims to characterize the mental differences among them, hoping in the end to throw light on ultimate problems of psychological analysis.   Instead of applying tests which yield an unequivocal *yes* or *no*, or *so much* or *so little*, it may even put problems which allow of widely different attempts at solution, of a number of possible kinds of errors, and of different methods of correcting these errors.   General observation is appealed to, and in all respects such work may utilize rougher data than would be possible in purely quantitative studies.

The study to be reported is distinctly of the latter, type.   It makes no attempt at psychophysical exactness and the establishment of mathematical correlations.   The ideal followed is shaped largely by such work as that of Hobhouse on animals and that of Binet in his "Experimental Study of Intelligence."

The fact that the study aims chiefly at intellectual to the neglect of emotional and volitional differences must not be construed as antagonistic to the voluntaristic trend of modern psychology.   On the contrary, I believe that the key to an explanation of the intellectual differences I have found lies often in native differences of emotional reaction.   The difficulty of the task and the lack of time have kept me to the narrower field.

What value can such a study have for psychological theory? In the first place it should throw some light on the problem of "general mental ability." Is intellectual ability (to adapt the figure of Lloyd Morgan to our purpose) a bank account, on which we can draw for any desired purpose, or is it rather a bundle of separate drafts, each drawn for a specific purpose and inconvertible? Let us review a few of the highly contradictory answers that have been given it.

Ebbinghaus says (5): "Wherever we look we find that mental ability (*Tüchtigkeit*) consists in something similar; only the material changes with which it works. It is the same with the learned man who is able to fill the gaps and explain the contradictions of historical material, as with the artist who elaborates our sense perception through a meaningful conception of the whole, or as with the skilled merchant who makes disposition of his goods in accordance with his means, the needs of the public, and political and social factors." Spearman (18, p. 284), after stating the approximately absolute correspondence which he finds between "General Discrimination" and "General Intelligence," says: "The above and other analogous observed facts indicate *that all branches of intellectual activity have in common one fundamental function (or group of functions), whereas the remaining or specific elements of the activity seem in every case to be wholly different from that in all the others.*" Again he says: "As an important practical consequence of this universal unity of the intellectual function, the various actual forms of mental activity constitute a stably interconnected Hierarchy according to their different degrees of intellective saturation."

Perhaps the most outspoken advocate of the opposite view is Thorndike (21). Basing his conclusions on the lack of correlation found between simple tests of the ability to do two or more apparently similar things, he says: "Good reasoning power is but a general name for a host of particular capacities, the general average of which seems to the namer to be above the general average in other individuals." Again, "the most hopeless scholar in one field will in another be not so very far below mediocrity. The discovery of the exact amount of the relationship thus disposes finally of the opinion that brightness is brightness and that those who possess it may use it equally well in any field."

In the last quotation, the controversy takes on the aspect of a dispute between nominalism and realism. To deny General Intelligence on the ground that it is made up of a host of particular abilities whose relative proportions vary from man to man, is like denying the existence of a distinctively human body on the ground that the relative proportions of its parts are not the same for any two individuals. The important question is one of fact and not of name. If an individual takes low rank in every mental performance it is immaterial whether we say his "General Intelligence" is low, or whether we say he is defective in this, that, and the other "particular ability." And there are undoubted cases of individuals who take such universally low rank. As a contribution of fact, then, our study should have some bearing on the question of General Intelligence.

Again, it seems that a comparative study of intellectual differences should throw some light on the relative importance, for intelligence, of such factors as memory, habit, attention, etc., each of which, more or less, is teased out and thrown into relief by the conditions of the study. Nearly every sort of mental operation has been at some time or other singled out by psychologists and set up as the leading element of intellectual ability.

My subjects were specially selected as among the brightest or most stupid that could be found in the public schools within easy distance of Clark University, in the city of Worcester. Three ward principals, by the aid of their teachers, made out a list of about two dozen boys of the desired age, equally divided between the two groups.[1]

These two dozen were selected from about 500 boys. Out of this list, fourteen were found who were willing to come to the University as often as desired for experimentation—seven bright and seven dull. They came singly, or sometimes in

---

[1] I am very greatly indebted to the principals and to the teachers as well, for their generous co-operation and particularly for the large amount of information they have given me concerning the school activities of my subjects.

pairs (according to the nature of the work), three or four times a week for one hour's work. To be more sure of regular attendance, they were promised a small fee for each visit, to be paid only in case they continued through all the exercises. This, however, would probably not have been necessary, as the confidence of the subjects was easily won, and the exercises were for the most part interesting and also quite out of the routine of their every day school-work. With a few exceptions, mentioned here and there in the results, the subjects gave every evidence of doing the best work they were capable of. Over much of it they were enthusiastic. Several of the subjects showed a good deal of interest and curiosity to know what ones were making the best records, and I had to be careful not to allow information to leak out that would discourage the poorer workers. By generously distributing praise, it was so managed that those whose work was almost uniformly poor never became aware of the fact.

All the work was done in the psychological laboratory of Clark University, except that with M and N, who spent about two hours at my home three to four evenings out of every week. In conversation and games, other than the tasks given, I had ample opportunity to get well acquainted with all. The trips made to the laboratory were at the following hours: 8 to 9. A. M.; 1 to 2 and 4 to 6 P. M. Altogether, I spent on an average about six hours per day, six days in the week, in personal contact with my subjects, singly or in pairs. This was begun about January 20th, 1905, and continued without intermission until May 10th following.

In making the selection of subjects, the teachers were asked simply for those they considered "brightest" or "dullest," in the ordinary significance of the terms. The only caution given was that their judgment should be based upon the child as a whole, and not simply upon his class work in the school subjects. In doing this it was not expected that the teacher's judgment would be infallible, but it was confidently expected that this method would afford two groups of subjects sufficiently distinct from each other for the purpose of a comparative study of intelligence. In this I was not disappointed. This procedure, however, has been criticised on the ground that the dullard at school often later shows himself efficient in life's activities. Such examples as Sir Walter Scott, Oliver Goldsmith, Patrick Henry, Wellington and General Grant have been frequently cited in support of this. No one would defend the school as a universally efficient test of mental ability, and yet the boy who with best effort cannot solve the school problems, who cannot master an ordinary vocabulary in his mother tongue or apply the simple rules of grammar, who sees no meaning to historical or scientific facts after honestly trying to comprehend them, is not likely to be distinguished later as a man of intelligence. In some cases, closer investigation shows that the poor school standing imputed to many famous men has been exaggerated or partially reported. And, finally, what the present paper is concerned with is the testing of boys now considered bright or dull, without reference to their future development.

In the beginning, then, we do not define "brightness" or "dullness" any more definitely than does the world in general. The aim was to secure subjects whom most people would readily agree in classifying one way or the other, and then proceed to the investigation of what constitutes the fundamental intellectual differences between the two groups. A large number of such studies ought to end by giving us a definition of terms. At present, such definitions are lacking.

A more specific criticism might be made on the ground that a good deal of my work was carried on at an unfavorable part of the day, particularly that between four and six in the afternoon, after the close of the school day. That this may have affected the results to a certain extent cannot be denied, but that it did so to any considerable extent is unlikely. First, because the afternoon session in the Worcester schools is less than two hours in length; second, because my experiments were for the most part interesting to the subjects and quite different from the routine of school work; and third, most important of all, because past experiments indicate that a short, interesting, mental task, given to pupils who are undoubtedly fatigued after a day of school work, does not give serious indication of the presence of such fatigue. Moreover, the afternoon subjects were equally divided between the two groups in order that the relative standing of the groups might not be affected. In passing, it may be noted that my best subject did his work between 4 and 5 P. M.

Perhaps the most unfavorable element in the conditions of the experiment is the age difference. The ages of the subjects when the work was begun were as follows:

BRIGHT GROUP (I).

A	B	C	D	E	F	G
10 yrs. 2 mos.	11 yrs. 1 mo.	10 yrs. 10 mos.	10 yrs. 5 mos.	10 yrs. 8 mos.	10 yrs. 7 mos.	11 yrs. 5 mos.

DULL GROUP (II).

H	I	J	K	L	M	N
13 yrs. 5 mos.	10 yrs. 4 mos.	10 yrs. 9 mos.	10 yrs. 11 mos.	12 yrs. 5 mos.	11 yrs.	13 yrs. 9 mos.

It is practically certain that our results are not exactly what they would have been if there had been no age discrepancy. It should be noted, however, that excepting N, H, and L the greatest age difference is fifteen months. And if we also except G and A, the greatest difference is only nine months. B, C, E, F, J, K and M are within six months of each other. It must also be noted that the largest age differences are so distributed as to give the advantage in maturity to the dull group. Such intellectual distinctions between the groups as do appear will therefore be more significant than they would have been if the age advantage had been on the other side; and somewhat more significant than if there had been no age difference at all.

It need only be stated at this point that the home life and general experience of the subjects present no very marked extremes. None were from extremely poor families or gave evidence of lack of nutritious food. They were all from respectable, middle-class homes, though of course showing different degrees of culture and refinement, to be noted in the general observations. (Section XI, below.) All the subjects live in one of the best portions of the city which, as a whole, is uncrowded, clean and generally devoid of squalor. They have had as nearly the same sort of school training as one could expect from pupils of a given district of a given city. I think it may be stated that in general the environmental conditions have been favorable to the study.

The ability of the fourteen boys above described was subjected to tests at eight more or less different points, to wit: (1) their powers of invention and creative imagination; (2) their logical processes; (3) their mathematical ability; (4) their mastery of language; (5) their insight, as shown in the interpretation of fables; (6) their ease of acquisition, as shown in learning to play chess; (7) their powers of memory; and (8) their motor ability both in general and in the acquisition of bodily skill. The tests upon each point were numerous and varied but constituted a connected group. The details with regard to the particular tests of each group and the results obtained will be found in the eight sections next following.

III. INVENTIVENESS AND CREATIVE IMAGINATION.

Before taking up the experiments concerned with these

processes let us consider for a moment their general scope and nature.

What do we mean by invention?   Otis T. Mason defines it as "every change in human activity made designedly and systematically" (14).   According to this broad definition, invention is the typical intellectual activity, being involved in the creation of language, in art, social activities, and philosophy. We have only to compare the negro with the Eskimo or Indian, and the Australian native with the Anglo-Saxon, to be struck by an apparent kinship between general intellectual and inventive ability.   Mason calls the great inventor an "epitome of the genius of the world."   Bain also (1, p. 337) points out that the great inventors are men of scientific calibre and that the greatest of experimentalists are inventors.   Paulhan (16) goes so far as to say that the inventions of the poet and artist do not differ at bottom from those of the scientist and philosopher.   Mach (13, p. 174) quotes approvingly a saying of Liebig to the same effect, and adds that "if it is the business of the artist to build up his work from a few motives, it is the task of science to discover the motives which permeate reality."   Likewise Mach asserts that the mechanical engineer is exercising much the same activities as the scientist, except that the riddles of the latter have more unknown terms and are less definitely put.   According to this view, to develop a dog from a wolf, a Krag-Jorgeson from a bow and arrow, a lucifer match from the primitive fire stick, has involved much the same activities as have been operative in transforming fetichism and magic into religion and philosophy, or scattered knowledge into science.   This theory derives a certain plausibility from the fact that mechanical inventions have grown up *pari passu* with the development of such great concepts as cause, number, time, space, etc.   They have kept pace roughly, also, with the development of the arts, philosophy, science and religion.   Such a parallelism in development is most easily explained by supposing the two phenomena dependent to a certain degree upon the same sort of mental processes, though doubtless many other factors are involved.

However this may be, it is clear that invention is largely dependent upon constructive imagination, the ability to abstract from present experience and picture new situations, their possibilities and their consequences.   In both, images are united intentionally in order to form a new combination.   It is imagination which invents.   Reason is only a mode of control and justification.   It determines values, accepts or rejects, but must get its raw material from creative imagination.   Conjecture, which is only another name for the same thing, is at the basis of the most diverse scientific inventions.   All sciences begin with hypotheses. All this means also the ability to profit by experience, to sift out the useful element from a manifold, to bring the past to bear upon the future, to join elements previously isolated.

It is reasonable to suppose that the decisive intellectu al differences among men are not greatly dependent upon native retentiveness or mere sense discrimination. Far more important than this mass of raw sense data is the correct shooting together of the sense elements in memory and imagination. This is invention. It is the synthetic or apperceptive activity that gives the "seven-league boots" to genius. It is a kind of ability that all great minds exhibit. Why so great spontaneous relating activity in one mind and so little in another, is the ultimate problem in this portion of individual psychology.

The opposite of invention is not imitation, but routine. The absence of routine implies often a certain disequilibrium, a mental activity irregular and perhaps uncoördinated. It is a breaking up of preferred associations. We may think of it as due to a nervous ferment, for it is in point of fact augmented by certain maladies, as phthisis and alcoholism. (16, p. 167.)

We have above presented the view that at bottom all invention is one and the same thing. We are able, nevertheless, to mark out three sorts of inventive genius that differ somewhat from each other. They are, first, *mechanical* invention, involving a type of creative imagination that is exact, clear, objective, concrete, with little of the affective element. Second, *artistic* invention which is more emotional, subjective and romantic. Its imagery is somewhat less perceptual or concrete than that of mechanical invention, and it is more characteristic of dreamy and myth-making minds. Third, *scientific* and *philosophical* invention, whose imaginative constructions are conceptual, schematic, abstract. This corresponds to Ribot's three-fold division of the creative imagination.

It is probable that these three sorts of invention look more alike from without than from within. That is to say, while much alike if viewed objectively, they have each a peculiar affective tone that will make success in one a hindrance to success in another. It is partly interest that makes one revel in one kind and apathetic toward another. In embryo they show more similarities, but diverge rapidly as tastes and interests become set.

In the tests about to be described ten problems or puzzles were given. In some, the puzzle aspect was largely removed by the statement of the problem or by a hint given in such a way as to help the subject over the portion that might otherwise be thought to render the problem a "catch." The purpose of these problems was two-fold. In the first place, it was expected that they would throw light on the differences in constructive imagination and the entire complex of activities that generally go under the name of invention. In the second place it was hoped they would reveal any differences that existed in the stage of development of the logical processes among the subjects. It was expected that such differences would show themselves in the methods of solution, the lower grade subjects adopting more the "method of trial and error" and giving more evidence generally of perceptual thought as opposed to conceptual. The last three are especially adapted to this end.

It may be objected that such problems as we have described below do not test real intellectual ability, but only a spurious kind which would better be denominated ingenuity, Yankee shrewdness, the *entrepreneur* spirit, or the ability which enables one *"se tirer d'affaire."* Without defending the thesis that such mental traits as are here called into play are faithfully indicative of mental ability in general, we may yet hold that they are so to a certain extent. Such, in the opinion of a recent writer, are the very qualities most necessary for the scientific research student. In the words of Professor Henry Shaler Williams (23), "The underlying principle of scientific research is simple inquisitiveness; that trait so characteristic of the Yankee and the fox. I use the term Yankee as the name for the smart, shrewd, inventive man, who depends upon his own resources, and if without learning or education, still succeeds in penetrating untried fields and in making headway under all manner of reverses, hindrances and difficulties, always exhibiting a quickness to observe differences and to interpret the meaning of things. All kinds of successful pioneers are made of such stuff." This trait of adaptability to environment would seem to constitute an important distinction between the higher and lower races. The Papuan is indigenous, the European is cosmopolitan.

All this, again, is in close harmony with Janet's recently expressed theory of brain levels. The three levels of Hughlings Jackson are replaced in this theory by five levels, the highest of which is not that concerned with conceptual and abstract thought, but the one that controls adjustment to immediate environment. With this highest level defective, one may be ever so learned and yet lack the chief elements that go to make up what the world regards as common sense. If the problems here presented appear trivial, it is due to our conventional modes of thought. In order to heighten our respect for even the slightest inventive genius we have only to glance at the slow and laborious processes in the development of all inventions. Engrossed in routine thinking for so long, most of us have lost our appreciation for naïve bits of originality. The book learning of the average educated man gives to his thought a routine and conventional setting that causes him to lose perspective. Such a person, struggling for university degrees and trying to master the current concepts of philosophy or science, begins after a while to fancy that his own sort of mental activity is of higher quality than the mechanic or artisan is engaged in.

Below is a statement of the first six problems, together with a description of the conditions and results for each. The other four will be considered in the following section on the Logical Processes.

Problem 1. A man has five short chains of three links each.

Show how he can put these five pieces together into one long chain by the use of only three weldings.

Conditions. The five pieces, made of small wire, were laid on the table side by side in front of the subjects. Care was taken to see that they understood what was wanted, after which they were asked to put the chains together. The problem offers two convenient places for assistance in case of failure. If the subject failed to discover within ten minutes that three links of one piece must be used as connecting links (as is necessary), then I opened such links and placed them before him near the other pieces. In most cases this hint was sufficient. When it was not, further help was given by placing the three open links in the proper positions.

Results. As given at first the problem may not be thought fair. The first point is really difficult to see. Only *D* and *L* were successful without any help, *D* within 30 seconds and *L* at the end of 4½ minutes. All the others, therefore, were assisted by my opening the three proper links. Thereupon *B*, *C*, *E*, *G* and *N* proceeded at once, within 30 seconds, to unite the other four pieces by means of them. *H*, *J*, and *K* also succeeded but only after further trials and errors, using 4, 2¼, and 4¾ minutes respectively. For *A*, *M*, and *I* the three links were not only opened but also placed in their proper positions between the pieces. Even then *A* and *I* did not get the idea, but continued fastening the links apparently without choice. Both failed in the 30 minutes allotted.

Of group II only *L* and *J* showed any noticeable tendency to study out the situation without actually placing and fastening the chains, while all the better group except *A* did so. In general, the attempts of group II were more rapidly made and the successive variations more trivial than those of group I. For example, if the first procedure was by fastening piece one to piece two and then to piece three, etc., the next attempt was likely to be by fastening one to five. That is, the essential point in the error was not grasped. Some in group I also started out in some cases with little more rationality, but with the exception of *A* they did not repeat an error so often in the same or slightly different form as did the boys in group II.

Problem 2. Fifteen matches were placed on the table so as to form the figure shown on the next page:[1] The subjects were asked to remove three matches and leave exactly three squares.

This test gives room for a certain amount of rational procedure. It is decidedly more rational to cast the eyes about to see what squares should be retained than simply to pick up

---

[1]Used by Miss Thompson: Mental Traits of Sex. Chicago, 1903. p. III.

4

three matches at random and then look to see whether three squares are left. Casual inspection will show that certain of

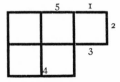

the matches, *e. g.*, 1, 2, 3, 4, etc., must remain. The eye must run over the figure rapidly to see what portions offer the most promise. Rapid combinations of different squares must be made. Certain matches must be thought out of existence.

Results. No one of group II succeeded in the 10 minutes allotted. E, B, and G of group I were successful in $3\frac{1}{2}$, 2 and $5\frac{1}{4}$ minutes respectively. The other subjects were assisted at the end of 10 minutes by having match 5 removed for them. M, L, and N finished in 2, $2\frac{1}{4}$ and 3 minutes respectively. The other four stupid subjects H, I, J, K, failed in the additional 5 minutes given. Of the remaining bright subjects, all succeeded : A in $4\frac{1}{2}$ minutes, F in $3\frac{3}{4}$ minutes, C in $2\frac{1}{4}$ minutes, D in 4 minutes. The tendency in general was to try matches that were adjacent or opposite. Only E, G, and B gave evidence of choosing squares rather than individual matches. It was also noticeable that of group II only L and M gave evidence of making any attempt other than by actual removal of matches, while all of group I, except A, did so. None of the subjects attempted a logical, mathematical solution like that suggested by Miss Thompson.

Problem 3. A man travelling with a fox, a goose, and some corn comes to a river. He can only take one over at once. If he leaves the fox and goose together, the goose will be eaten. If he leaves the goose and corn together, the corn will be eaten. How can he mange to get them all safely over ?

Conditions. The subject was provided with small wooden blocks of different shapes representing the different objects. These he carried over a book (representing a river) to demonstrate the solution. To solve this puzzle alone rquires a good deal of ingenuity. The important idea, of course, is that of carrying the goose back. This is in the nature of a "catch," and did not occur to any of my subjects. After 10 minutes of unsuccessful trials it was explained that it would be allowable for the man to carry any of them over and back again if he cared to do so. Five minutes more were then allotted. In case of failure again, they were then instructed that the goose was the proper one to carry back.

Results. None of the subjects were successful without assistance. After the first bit of instruction, all but E of group I, and H and J of group II were successful. The remaining ones were successful after the second bit of assistance. It is interesting to note how quickly the pupils learned that the solution must begin by the man carrying the goose over. This is the first essential point, and was seen at once by all except E, I, K and N. These continued their false starts for some time even after they had been found to lead to failure. The ingenious, "smart" suggestions nearly all came from J, K, and M. Some of these are as follows: "separate them on the opposite bank," "hurry back before the fox can eat the goose up," "let the fox swim over," "call the fox over," "put the corn in his pocket," "throw the corn over," "hide the corn," "tie up the fox," etc. This may signify a greater difficulty for these subjects in comprehending the conditions of the problem, or a greater aversion to making any serious effort at doing so.

Problem 4. Two boys and two men are travelling and come to a river which has no bridge and is too deep to wade. None of them can swim. They find a small boat which will carry two boys or one man. How can they manage it so that all may get over?

Conditions. The subjects were given a toy boat and blocks representing boys and men. Each was allowed to keep trying not only till successful but till the process was completely learned and could be gone through without error.

Results. The following shows the time in minutes spent by each subject in actual trials before all the errors were avoided. Time spent between successive trials is not counted.

GROUP I.

A	B	C	D	E	F	G
7.27	1.36	1.58	2.20	5.41	x	5.25

GROUP II.

H	I	J	K	L	M	N
1.15	9.25	5	10.33	2.45	9.27	17.47

The total number of errors for group I was 35, distributed among six subjects (F was not tested), A and E being responsible for 20 of them. For group II there were 87, K, M, and N having 61.

The most frequent error in both groups was that of a man going over and coming back at once, and the next that of a boy going over alone.

The following shows the number of trials made by each subject before all errors were avoided.

GROUP I.

A	B	C	D	E	F	G
6	1	3	3	5	x	1

GROUP II.

H	I	J	K	L	M	N
2	8	5	14	3	8	10

After the subject had learned the moves using the blocks he was told to close his eyes and describe the necessary moves orally. All were able to do this without hesitation except *M*, who made several errors.

Thereupon the subject was allowed to close his eyes while I named the moves orally. Then I would stop suddenly and have him state the situation resulting from my instructions. *I*, *K*, and *M* had great difficulty in this, being able to follow only short, simple moves.

There are several factors that make for success in this problem. The effect of various possible moves may be pictured in advance by imaging the blocks in other positions than those which they occupy. It may be objected that even the subjects able to do this will not do so, but rather depend on lucky moves to bring it around all right in the end. It is true that in some cases boys of group I do begin with haphazard moving. But the significant fact is that they abandon this procedure after a few moves for one which is more rational. Instead of making a trial and letting the result tell whether it is correct, they try to foresee what will result from a contemplated move.

It may be objected also that a subject may be successful simply because of making a lucky move early in the test and then repeating it mechanically. But here is an important point. Certain of the subjects, when successful by accident, stopped to find out the cause of the good fortune. Certain others went on repeating the old errors or making new ones. The table shows the marked inferiority, generally speaking, of group II on this test. But in no case was the procedure entirely haphazard. Even the poorest cases, as a rule, began by taking over two boys. The most obvious possible errors were hardly made at all. This partial avoidance of the trial and error method shows that the subjects were really employing their intellectual capabilities in solving the problem. Whether they were doing so to their utmost, it is impossible to determine.

After solving the above problem the subjects were asked to show how seven men and two boys could get across the river in this same boat. All were successful at the first attempt except *H* and *K*, who succeeded on the second trial. *B*, *G*, and *C* volunteered the information that any number of men could be taken across that way.

Problem 5. A mother sent her boy to the river to get four pints of water. She gave him only two vessels, one holding three pints, the other five pints. The boy must bring exactly four pints, no more, no less. How shall he measure it?

Conditions. The subject was given vessels of the proper sizes and taken to the tap to demonstrate the solution. In order to avoid all unfairness it was explained that the boy would be allowed to pour water from vessel to vessel as much as he desired. Since the measuring may be begun by filling either vessel first, uniform conditions were secured by instructing each subject to begin with the three pint vessel. There are then the following steps to go through: 1. Fill the three pint vessel and empty it all into the other. 2. Fill the three pint vessel again and empty out two pints by filling the other full. 3. Empty the large vessel and use it to save the one pint remaining in the small vessel. 4. Fill up the small vessel again.

In case of failure at the end of 10 minutes the subject was reminded of the two pint space left in the large vessel after the three pints had been put in. Then if unsuccessful after ten minutes he was carried through step 2 above. If unable to proceed after ten minutes more, step 3 was given.

Results. None succeeded without assistance. *B*, *D*, *G* and *J* were able to proceed after being simply reminded of the two pint space. *H* and *L* were able to work out the last two steps alone while all the other subjects were able to get only the last step. Although it was very carefully explained that guessing would not be allowed and that the water must really be measured, nevertheless certain of the subjects could not be made to omit it. By "guessing" is meant any attempt to get a particular amount without actually measuring it. *A*, *E*, *I*, *K*, *M* and *N* were especially prone to this procedure. When one sort of "guessing" was forbidden they would try another. *B*, *D*, *F* and *G* refrained from it after being reminded once or twice. Generally speaking, the subjects of group II made far more useless trials than did those of group I.

The problem, considering the assistance given at the beginning, is entirely fair and gives room for a good deal of ingenuity. A distant end must be kept in mind and various possible combinations tried in order to see whether they further this end.

Problem 6. The subject was given six pennies and told to arrange them in two rows of four pennies each. If not successful in 10 minutes he was told that it was allowable to place one penny on top of another if he cared to do so.

Result.   *F* and *J* were successful without help.   The others failed in the 10 minute period and were given the above mentioned assistance.   Thereupon all succeeded within five minutes, except *A*, *M*, and *N*.   With this puzzle, group I made many more trials than group II.   *A*, *C*, and *G*, especially, made their combinations very rapidly, while *F*, *J*, *K*, *L* and *M* made few trials.

Constructive imagination in Chess.   The details concerning the chess test are given in Section VIII, but since ability to plan the game is closely associated with invention and constructive imagination I have incorporated the ranking in chess playing with the ranking for the tests of this section in Table I.[1]

TABLE I.

Grading and Ranking of Subjects on Tests of Inventiveness.

Problem.	1	2	3	4	5	6	Chess.	Composite Ranking.
A	5	2	2	4	3	1	3	10
B	2	1	1	1	1	2	1	1
C	2	2	1	2	2	2	2	4
D	1	2	1	2	1	2	3	3
E	2	1	2	3	3	2	3	9
F	3	2	2	3	2	1	3	7
G	2	1	1	1	1	2	2	2
H	3	3	1	1	2	2	3	5
I	5	3	2	4	3	2	4	11
J	3	3	1	3	1	1	4	7
K	3	3	3	5	3	2	5	13
L	1	2	2	2	2	2	4	5
M	4	2	3	5	3	3	5	14
N	2	2	2	5	3	3	4	11

Table I gives a summary of the results of Section III so far as they concern the relative ability of the individuals tested.   The method employed was to assign to each boy a grade on the scale of 3 or of 5 as

---

[1] That our puzzle-problems really did involve constructive imagination is indicated by the close correlation found between the rankings that they give and that for chess, which involves the latter in a high degree.

the precision of the test permitted, 1 being the highest mark. The composite ranking is calculated by summing the grades given for the individual tests and assigning a new mark in accordance with the sums obtained, the rank 1 being assigned to the boy having the lowest total, and so on. In case the sum of the grades for the individual test turned out the same for any two boys, both were given the same rank and the next rank number was omitted altogether. In Table I, for example, H and L are both ranked 5 in the composite ranking, and rank 6 is omitted; in the same way F and J are ranked 7 and the rank 8 is omitted.

On the basis of this table we are able to throw our subjects into five groups according to their inventive ingenuity (of the mechanical type). 1. B and G, who are almost uniformly good. 2. C, D, H and L. 3. E, F, and J, who are rather irregular. 4. A and N. 5. I, K, and M, who stand distinctly lowest.

The second and third kinds of invention have barely been touched by my experiments, but several important points have come out incidentally. For example, as mentioned elsewhere, C is distinctly of artistic temperament, with a passion for drawing and painting and a marked liking for works of fiction. N belongs to the lively, imaginative, unstable type of stupidity distinguished by Kraepelin from the dull type. L is somewhat of the same type but less distinctly so, and frequently rises out of the stupid class. H, I, J, K and M approach Kraepelin's dull type, and show little invention of any kind. B and G show the highest development of the power in question. Their inventive ability belongs rather to the mechanical sort.

As a group, the duller boys make many trials with slight variations and do not study the situation before attacking it, both of which characteristics testify to their feeble ability to present to themselves anything beyond what actually lies before them. They tend, like the animals, to live in a world of immediate sense experience.

Well chosen puzzle problems seem to the writer to furnish a satisfactory general test for imagination of the every day practical sort. It is clear, however, that subjects of good ability may fail in one or two special cases, and subjects of poor ability succeed, so that the test should be carried out with a sufficiently varied assortment of similar problems. The tests throw much light also on methods of logical procedure, and will be considered in this respect at the close of the next section.

IV. THE LOGICAL PROCESSES.

The second series of puzzles was devised to throw light on the degree of development of the logical processes, to get at differences in methods of mastering intellectual difficulties.

No doubt the broad outlines of this phase of mental development are familiar to the reader. It is a matter of common information that the lowest forms of life profit little or not at all by experience, and that the ability so to do has been generally agreed upon as the best criterion of a conscious life. The classic example of Möbius's pike may be taken as representative of the next higher stage. The pike ceases his efforts to devour the small fish after he has half killed himself by bruising his head against the plate glass that separates them from him. He also leaves them undisturbed even after the partition has been removed. No other adaptability is shown. In other words we have an example of associative memory, but one very difficult to stamp in.

The higher animals, such as the rat, or monkey, show vastly increased ability to reach a desired end through memory of success and error. The problem is attacked in a haphazard way until accident brings success. If rational processes were very effective here the animal would look about for the cause of his success and thereafter avoid error and discard superfluous movements. As a matter of fact this is not the case; errors and useless movements are eliminated only gradually and in proportion as the successful activities become more firmly grounded in neural structure as habit. The typical curve of learning, then, by the "trial and error method" is one of *gradual* descent. This is the sort of learning characteristic of animal intelligence.

The logic of the learning processes in children has been studied experimentally by Hodge (7), Lindley (11), and Kinnaman (9). They show that the methods of young children in approaching a problem are essentially like those of the rat or monkey, namely a series of haphazard trials, a lucky accident, and gradual elimination of the useless efforts. But a significant fact is that the curve presents a steeper descent than is the case with animals. Error may be repeated, but not so often. The work of Lindley shows that at about the ages of ten or twelve the "trial and error method" is giving place to a more rational procedure. "The lack of circumspection, the conventional beginnings, the automatic repetition of former movements, the slight and inconsequential variations, the frequent relapses into routine after failure of a slight variation, in short, the general tardiness in profiting by errors, of children of grade III, slowly makes way in older children for greater prevision, more adequate analysis of design, less conventionality and automatism in procedure, more radical reconstruction of plans in successive trials, all of which leads to greater promptness in profiting by mistakes." (11, p. 469.) Kinnaman's experiments show a similar improvement in the adult as compared to the child. They are able, also, to learn by the experience of others as well as by their own.

But we need not break off our comparison at this point. Adults themselves show the greatest differences in this respect. The noted inventors and the experimentalists have shown ability to profit by error and happy chance far surpassing that of the ordinary person, intricate errors often being second in importance only to truth itself. For the scientist, negative results may be almost as valuable as positive. The history of invention is a record of success built upon failure.

To sum up the course of development just traced, we may follow the example of Mezes (15) and lay down three tolerably well defined stages. 1. "Trial and error." 2. Action that is purposive, but not chosen. 3. Action that is purposive and chosen. To animals Thorndike grants the first only, and asks us to close the question on his decision. On the other hand, Hobhouse seems to prove that certain animals, at least, partake of the second grade. No one, however, would ascribe to them the third sort. As pointed out by Mezes, they may know that a certain action produces a certain result, but not why. They do not scrutinize a situation with a view to discover the best mode of procedure. "They do not even ask *double* questions, still less *general* ones." The reasoner, morever, breaks up a problem into its parts, while the monkey, the child, or the stupid man deals with it as a whole and is soon balked. The reasoner hunts for his error, the animal only knows that the trial was unsuccessful; it does not ask why. Our fourteen boys present a tolerably long scale of differences in this particular.

The following is a summary of the results gained with them from the four puzzles bearing upon this question.

Problem 7. A ball is lost in a round field. The grass is so tall that you can only see ten feet on each side of you. Show what path you would take in looking for the ball.[1]

Results. The subject was given pencil and a piece of paper on which was a circle to represent the field. They fall, according to procedure, into four groups. 1. Those who began at the circumference and circled round and round spirally to the center. This includes C, E, F, G, H and L. 2. B and A began at the edge and marked across from side to side in parallel lines until the whole field was covered. 3. K and N marked out a path that resembled somewhat the shape of a wheel with spokes, but was more irregular. 4. D, I, J and M ran the pencil about apparently at haphazard until the whole circle was marked over.

---

[1] This problem is borrowed from Dr. C. F. Hodge.

Problem 8. Trace the following figure without crossing a line, lifting the pencil, or tracing any part twice.

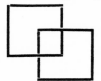

Results. A, B, C, D, E, F, H, K and L succeeded the first trial, G, I, M and N the second trial, and J the fourth.

The solution, of course, is very simple and cannot be missed if the tracer looks at all ahead of his pencil. It will be noted that only one of group I, but four of group II, failed at the first attempt. This may reasonably be interpreted as indicating a greater tendency in the stupid subjects toward what has been called perceptual thinking. Instead of the action being governed by an end, each stage of the process is motivated mechanically by the preceding stage.

Problem 9. Trace the following figure without lifting the pencil and without retracing.[1]

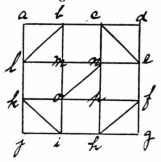

The following table shows the time, the number of trials, and the starting places for each subject.

Subjects.	A	B	C	D	E	F	G	H	I	J	K	L	M	N
Number of trials,	7	6	5	2	11	10	3	4	8	12	11	13	4	3
Time in minutes,	30	17	21	6	38	53	7	8	30	41	23	37	28	8
Starting points in order,	a g a g c g n	j j j j j o	b a a d n	j n	e g g h i i i i i o	e d c d d d i i a n	h a o	a j k o	j a d a g a a n	a l p p g a b a a p p n	j f f f f i f f l o	a a a a a a a a a n	a a a n	j j o
Grade on scale of 3.	2	2	2	1	3	3	1	1	2	3	3	3	1	1

[1] Taken from Lindley: A Study of Puzzles: *American Journal of Psychology*, July, 1897, p. 461.

The table shows very frequent repetition of the same error in subjects *E*, *K*, and *L*. Out of the total of 44 trials for the bright subjects there are possible 37 changes of starting point. 21 changes were made—a percentage of 56+. The percentage of change in starting point was only 39+ for the stupid group. This difference corresponds to that found by Lindley between young and older children. In general my results on this test are so similar to age differences found by Lindley that we need not describe them in detail. They may be summed up by saying that subjects who did best showed less repetition of errors, and a tendency to make variations of a more radical nature, when at all. I may say, however, that the groups fell less radically apart in this test than I had anticipated.

Problem 10. Five circles were marked out thus on cardboard:

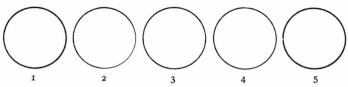

Black checker-men were placed on 1 and 2, and white ones on 4 and 5. The problem is to make the black and white men exchange positions. A piece may move forward one step or

TABLE II.

Times, trials and relapses with problem 10.

	Five circles.			Seven circles.			Nine circles.			Eleven circles.			Thirteen circles.			Grading on scale of five.
	Time.	Trials.	Relapses.	Time.	Trials.	Relapses.	Time.	Trials.	Relapses.	Time.	Trials.	Relapses.	Time.	Trials.	Relapses.	
A	3+	5	0	21+	36	2	No further trouble.									3
B	1+	3	0	1+	3	1	No further trouble.									1
C	7+	28	4	2+	6	1	5	0	No furth. trouble.							3
D	4½	10	1	6	7	1	3	0	No furth. trouble.							3
E	1⅓	4	1	16	25	2	2	0	No furth. trouble.							3
F	2	6	0	9¾	15	0	No further trouble.									2
G	4+	11	3	1½	2	0	No further trouble.									2
H	16+	30	4	19+	50	5	11	4		4	1	.	3	0		5
I	6+	12	3	11+	16	1	4	0		13	3	No trouble				4
J	15+	34	5	7+	19	2	24	5	No furth. trouble.							4
K	17+	28	7	12+	18	3	13	3		2	0		2	0		5
L	14+	22	4	21	26	6	No further trouble.									3
M	49	24	6	32	35	6	16	2	No furth. trouble.							4
N	3+	6	1	30	42	5	8	2	No furth. trouble.							4

jump over one piece, but cannot move backwards. After the solution for this was learned, seven circles were given with three men at each end. Afterward, nine circles with four men, then eleven circles with five men, then thirteen circles with six men at each end. As in all the other tests, record was kept of every move. The table above shows the chief facts in the results.

Time is represented in minutes. It was not kept for the nine circles trial, or those succeeding. Number of trials means the number after which no error was made for five successive trials. The number does not, however, include these five final and successful trials. By "relapse" is meant falling back into error after having been successful.

The above table shows in a striking degree the difference in the ability of the boys in grasping and generalizing the essential features of a method of procedure.

The following is my estimate of the composite ranking of the boys for the tests on the degree of development in logical procedure.

GROUP I.

A	B	C	D	E	F	G
5	1	3	6	8	4	2

GROUP II.

H	I	J	K	L	M	N
10	12	13	14	7	11	9

As before, E and L tend to depart from the group to which they were originally assigned.

Taking into consideration the whole group of ten problems—those described in the previous section as well as those just considered—we may say that the boys of the better group showed not only superior power of imagination but also a stronger tendency to psychical economy; they used their eyes instead of their fingers; or, going still further in the same direction, they experimented mentally instead of by actual manipulations; they studied things out before they began to operate; they tended to abstract from the particular problem and to announce general rules. When, as often happened, they began in a haphazard manner, they more quickly eliminated their errors, and in adopting new lines of procedure chose them less at random. They were at times interested to seek the causes of their successes. In general, the more poorly endowed may be expected to make more trials than the better endowed; but in a case where no clue presents itself readily, as for example in the case of Problem 6, and the better endowed are brought down also to the fumbling stage, the latter will probably be found to make the greater number of attempts. *B* and *G* showed the greatest advancement in logical procedure, abstraction, general range of knowledge and interpretation of it.

These problems, with perhaps the exception of Problem 8, seem well suited to their purpose. The last is eminently adapted for bringing out differences in degree of rationality of procedure. In several respects it is the most significant of the puzzle problems.

V. Differences in Mathematical Ability.

Ethnology shows that racial progress has been closely paralleled by development of the ability to deal with mathematical concepts and relations. Child psychology shows the same for individual development. This parallelism hinges on the importance of abstraction as a kind of intellectual short-hand. Without it we are helpless in mathematics and all else.

It was thought advisable, therefore, to investigate pretty closely the mathematical ability of my subjects. Eight sets of problems were given, involving more or less different phases of mathematical ability. Following we have a statement of the sorts of problems and a brief summary of the results with each sort.

1. *Mastery of the fundamental processes.* Fifteen problems were given, such as the following:

I.
(1) $2 + 2 + 2 + 2 - 3 - 2 + 3 = ?$
(2) $3 - 1 + 2 + 1 + 5 - 2 - 1 = ?$
(3) $1 + 4 - 2 + 4 - 1 - 1 + 2 = ?$

II. Fifteen slightly more difficult, such as
(1) $4 + 6 - 3 + 8 + 2 - 4 - 3 = ?$
(2) $5 - 4 + 8 + 3 - 6 + 5 - 2 = ?$
(3) $7 + 2 + 3 + 3 - 5 + 2 - 4 = ?$

III. Fifteen, of which the following are samples.
(1) $2 + 3 - 1 \times 2 - 3 + 1 \div 2 = ?$
(2) $4 - 2 - 1 + 3 \times 3 - 3 \div 3 = ?$
(3) $1 + 6 - 2 \times 3 - 5 \div 2 - 3 = ?$

Conditions. As in most of the other work, the subjects were taken singly. The problems were read aloud by me at a uniform rate and the subject called out the answer aloud.

Pencil and paper were not allowed. Ten seconds were taken for reading each problem in the first list, twelve for the second list, and fifteen for the third. Full records were kept of the time required for answering each problem.

Results. Wide differences appear, generally speaking, between the two groups. The subjects may be classified as follows: *A*, *B*, *C*, *E*, *F* and *G* made no more than three errors out of the 45 problems and omitted none at all. *D* and *L* either omitted or answered incorrectly 6. *H*, *I*, *K* and *N* omitted or answered incorrectly between 10 and 16. *J* and *M*, 26 and 29 respectively. As to *time* required, *A*, *B*, *C*, *D*, *E*, *F*, *G* and *L* gave their answers with practically no delay; *H*, *I*, *J*, *K* and *N* with delay usually of 5 to 15 seconds; *M*, 30 to 50, seconds.

2. *Fractions.*

(1)	Ten problems such as:	What is ½ of 8?,	⅓ of 12?
(2)	Ten such as : What is		⅓ of 18?, ¼ of 20?
(3)	" " " " "		⅔ of 8?, ¾ of 16?
(4)	" " " " "		⅓ of 16?, ¼ of 19?
(5)	Five " " " "		⅔ of 31?, ¾ of 11?

Conditions were the same as in the former problems; I read the problem, the subject gave the answer without the aid of pencil or paper. *Results.* *A*, *B*, and *G* were able to solve all the different kinds of problems given, and gave incorrect answers to no more than 5. *F*, *D*, and *L* were unable to solve those of the last list, and gave between 1 and 4 incorrect answers in the other lists. *E* and *C* could not solve those of the last list and missed 10 and 16 respectively among the others. *H*, *N*, and *I* could solve none in the last two groups, *K* and *J* none in the last three, and *M* could do nothing with any after the first group. According to *time* we have, four distinct groups. 1. *B*, *F*, and *G* very quick. 2. *A*, *D*, *L*, *E*, *J*, *C* distinctly slower. 3. *H*, *I*, *N* and *K*. 4, *M*, by far the slowest of all, his average time for the simple problems of the first list of fractions being more than 18 seconds.

3. *Changing money.* Twenty problems were given, such as the following. How much money should I receive if I buy an article that costs (1) 35 cents and I give the clerk 50 cents?

(2) 14	"	"	"	"	25 " ?
(3) 69	"	"	"	"	$1 ?
(4) 40	"	• "	"	"	$1 ?

Results. *A*, *B*, *F*, *G*, *N* were correct in all cases. *D*, *E*, *L*, *C* and *H*, answered incorrectly two to four times each. *I*, *K*, *J* and *M* answered incorrectly between six and ten times. As to *time*, five groups are readily distinguishable. 1. *B*. 2. *F*, *G*, *C*, *L*. 3. *A*, *D*, *E*. 4. *H*, *J*, *K*, *N*. 5. *I*, *M*.

4. *Conception of the simple mathematical relations of chance.* Twenty problems were given, of which the following is a sample. Twenty purses are lying on the table, all are empty except one, which contains $20, but you have no idea which one it is that contains the money. How much could you afford to give to be allowed to draw one of the purses. In the other problems the amount of money and the number of empty

and filled purses were changed about so that it soon became perfectly evident whether the relations involved were grasped.

Results. 1. $A, B,$ and G gave the correct answers to all. 2. C, E, H and N gave answers varying roughly but not exactly according to the conditions; most, however, being incorrect. 3. D and F varied their answers very slightly according to the conditions, practically all being incorrect. 4. $I, J, K, L, M,$ showed no comprehension at all of the relations. For example, $J,$ after a few problems, settled on $1.00 as the answer for all. When asked why he answered $1.00 for all the problems, he said, "Because that ain't much." K and L always estimated the worth of a draw at a little less than the sum contained in the purse; the former because "you are sure to earn 50 cents if you draw it," the latter because "If you draw it then you are $1.00 ahead."

5. *Problems involving the relations of measuring vessels.* This division included the following nine problems:

(1)	With a	7 and a	5 pint vessel	how	measure	out	10 pints?		
(2)	"	"	"	"	"	"	"	9	"
(3)	"	"	"	"	"	"	"	8	"
(4)	"	7 and 11	"	"	"	"	13	"	
(5)	"	"	"	"	"	"	"	15	"
(6)	"	"	"	"	"	"	"	10	"
(7)	"	13 and 9	"	"	"	"	17	"	
(8)	"	"	"	"	"	"	"	14	"
(9)	"	"	"	"	"	"	"	18	"

These problems are of exactly the same form as that coming under division 5 of the puzzle group. For that one, however, quite a different sort of mental ability is demanded than for the problems here given. For these, no vessels were supplied, but only the numbers representing the size of the vessels, together with pencil and paper. Since the boys now understood the general nature of these problems the puzzle aspect was no longer present. The solutions, however, are still of sufficient complexity to demand careful attention. Rapid combinations must be made, and as there are usually several steps in the solution, the result of the first stages of the process must be kept in mind while the last stages are being completed.

Results. A, B, C, D and G solved each within the five minutes allotted. E failed on one, F and J on two, I and N on three, H and K on four, L on five, and M on seven. The *time* is here very significant. B finished eight of his solutions in less than one minute each, D seven, A six, C and E five, G four, J and F three, $H, L,$ and N two, K and M one, and I none.

6. *Problems involving the sharing of expenses.* This was a

series of three problems, and, like most of the other series, of increasing difficulty. (1) *A* hires a carriage for $4.00 to drive to town and back. When half way there he overtakes *B* who wishes to ride with him. *A* allows him to do so on condition that *B* will share half of what the carriage costs for the distance he rides. How much does *B* owe *A* if he rides on to town and then back to the half-way spot where *A* took him in? (2) Same kind of problem except that the carriage cost only $1.50 and instead of taking in only one man he took in two, each of whom was to pay his share for the portion of the journey he rode. In the 3rd problem the cost of the carriage was $12.00, while *B* and *C* were taken in after one-fourth of the journey had been made.

Conditions. In order to avoid the difficulties in the wording of the problems, I illustrated them with paper and pencil as follows:

✕	△	✕
A's home	Where *B* got in	Town

Whole cost of carriage $4.00

The other problems were objectified similarly, and care was taken to repeat the statement until the subject understood the conditions, or until it was seen that he had not the ability to do so. When the solution was not reached within 10 minutes I gave a suggestion by pointing out what the entire cost of the carriage would be from the point where *B* entered, on to town, and back again to the same point. In case the solution was not reached within ten minutes more, I myself explained the solution to the subject very carefully and then allowed him to try the succeeding problem.

Results. 1. *A*, *B*, *C* and *G* solved all without help. 2. *D* and *E* failed on all in the allotted 10 minutes, but succeeded after the above mentioned suggestion was given them. 3. *F*, *L*, and *N* solved none, but gave some evidence of understanding the solution after it was explained to them. 4. *H*, *I*, *J*, *K* and *M* apparently understood nothing even after careful and repeated explanation.

7. *Problems involving the cost of two articles.* This group contains a list of seven problems. (1) I bought a bottle and a cork for $1.10; the bottle cost $1 more than the cork; how much did the cork cost? (2) I bought a horse and colt for $150, the horse costing $100 more than the colt. Find cost of the colt. The other five problems were analogous to these. The last one, however, involved a fraction and deserves special notice. (7) I bought a violin and bow for $20.00, the violin costing $15.00 more than the bow. Find the cost of the bow. This problem was inserted as a test to indicate whether or not the previous solution had been by rational procedure or simply

by trying different numbers until a combination was found that would satisfy the conditions of the problem. Pencil and paper were forbidden. When a solution was not reached in 10 minutes I explained the problem to the subject, and then let him proceed with the next in the list.

Results. Only two subjects solved the first problem, *A* and *G*. After the first, *A, B, D, E* and *G* had practically no difficulty, answering each within a few seconds. *L* and *N* also solved all after the first problem, but only after a good deal of fumbling on each one. *H, I, J, K* and *M* were as far from a solution of the last as of the first, although I did my best to explain each solution to them before setting them to the next. *C* had to be told the second, and thereafter had no difficulty. *F* failed on the second and also the last, showing that he had not evolved any rule.

8. *Problem involving the development of a rule.* I took a sheet of paper, folded it twice, in opposite directions, cut off the doubly folded corner, and before unfolding the paper, asked the subject to state the number of holes my cutting had made. After receiving the answer I unfolded the paper and allowed the subject to see whether or not his answer was correct. Then another sheet was folded similarly three times and the subject's answer to the same question recorded. The same was repeated for four, five, six and seven foldings. The rule in question is, of course, that the number of holes made by cutting off the corner of the folded sheet is doubled by increasing the number of folds by one.

Results. *B, C,* and *D* made no error. *A* made no error after the third trial, *G* none after the fourth trial, *L* got the last one correct, while the others, including *E, F, H, I, J, K, M* and *N* gave incorrect answers to all.

The following table summarizes the results for mathematical ability.

TABLE III.

Ranking for Mathematical Tests.

Sorts of questions.	1	2	3	4	5	6	7	8	Rank.
A	1	1	1	1	1	1	1	2	1
B	1	1	1	1	1	1	2	1	1
C	1	2	2	2	2	1	3	1	4
D	2	2	2	4	1	2	2	1	5
E	2	2	2	4	2	2	2	5	7
F	1	2	1	3	2	3	3	5	6
G	1	1	1	1	1	1	1	3	3

5

TABLE III.—*Continued.*

Sorts of ques-tions.	1	2	3	3	5	6	7	8	Rank.
H	4	4	2	2	4	4	5	5	10
I	4	4	5	5	3	5	5	5	12
J	5	4	4	5	3	5	4	5	11
K	4	4	4	5	4	5	5	5	12
L	3	2	2	5	4	3	3	4	8
M	5	5	5	5	5	5	5	5	14
N	3	4	2	4	3	3	3	5	9

It is worth noticing that in these tests E and L do not depart from the groups to which they were assigned by their teachers. It suggests that rapidity and precision in number work may be a considerable factor in "brightness" in the school sense of the word. It is true, also, that with tests of this sort the amount of school training is apt to be a factor. Such problems, nevertheless, make demands upon the powers of logical and abstract thought and are not without value as a test of these matters. Upon such problems Hancock based his study of the reasoning powers of children.

VI. LANGUAGE.

It is useless to insist on language as an index of intellectual development. Language is not only the expression, but also the *sine qua non* of conceptual thought proper. Every stage of a child's development has its peculiar language interests and language capabilities. Perhaps more than any other one class of facts, language growth epitomizes the development of a child's intelligence as a whole. My observations in this field include 1 Reading, 2 Building words from given letters, 3 Correction of mutilated text, 4 Spelling, 5 Fluency of expression and 6 Facility in obeying oral commands.

1. *Reading.* The subjects were given an easy and interesting story about 600 words in length to read aloud. They were simply asked to read as well as they were able. Careful notes and gradings were made. Following is a summary of the results :

TABLE IV.
Records from Reading Tests.

	Grade.	Time.	Words not pronounced correctly.	GENERAL REMARKS.
A	2	5½	0	Fluent, fairly expressive, a little monotonous, voice not very strong, no repetition, no hesitation, no mispronunciation, easy to follow. Gets B at school on reading.

TABLE IV.—*Continued.*

	Grade.	Time.	Words not pronounced correctly.	GENERAL REMARKS.
B	1	4¾	0	Modulation almost perfect, no repetition, no mispronunciation, reads with more expression than do most educated adults, could read at 4½ years of age and at 6 could read anything. Gets A at school.
C	1	4½	0	Voice pitched rather high, very much expression, emphasis a little overdone, slight stammering now and then with repetition of one or two words, hesitates once in a while apparently to let thought catch up with language. A to B at school.
D	2	4¼	0	Very much expression, no repetition, no mispronunciation, emphasis placed almost perfectly, matter of fact tone of voice. Gets A to B at school.
E	3	4¾	4	Hesitates some, fair expression, voice soft and attractive, emphasis well placed. Gets A to B at school
F	2	4	0	No hesitation or mispronunciation, monotony of voice is worst fault, thought seems to run ahead of language now and then. Gets A at school.
G	1	3½	0	A little monotonous, rather too rapid, no hesitation, no mispronunciation, emphasis good. Gets A to B at school. (G is in grade 8 at school and his school rank is thus gained by comparison with pupils more advanced than most of mine.)
H	4	6	11	Voice husky and nasal, very monotonous, poor emphasis and expression, reads sentence by sentence as though they were disconnected. Gets C at school.
I	3	5¼	2	Fair expression, tolerably fluent, little mispronunciation, emphasis misplaced here and there, voice rather subdued, no hesitation. Gets B— at school. Likes reading.
J	4	6½	6	Tolerably fluent, stopped three or four times to spell words, voice rather coarse and monotonous, emphasis not often misplaced. Gets C at school. Likes reading.
K	4	8½	9	Slow, hesitating, apparently takes in only a small portion at once, unable to read fluently through short sentences, voice monotonous, emphasis misplaced often. Gets C at school.
L	3	5	1	Tolerably fluent, fairly good emphasis, little mispronunciation, repetition now and then. Gets B to C at school. Likes to read.
M	4	9	5	Very slow and hesitating, runs over punctuation marks, expression and emphasis not so very bad. Gets C at school. Dislikes reading.
N	5	15	51	Voice pitched high and wholly unnatural, extraordinarily monotonous, sing-song tone, very slow and halting, spells over about one-third to one-half the words, misplaces emphasis, pays little heed to punctuation. By far my poorest reader. Gets D at school.

For two weeks I tutored *N* daily one hour in reading. His reading is by small units. Phrases are apparently not thrown together into one mental content. I made special effort to correct this fault, thinking it possibly only a matter of habit, but with little success. In making the effort to read by larger wholes he miscalls and transposes very many words. I had also little success in trying to get him to tone his voice down to conversational pitch and to modulate it more naturally. Punctuation was little heeded. He has a very marked habit of reversing the position of words in a phrase and of separate sounds in a word. Very often he hits correctly on part of the sound of a word and fills in the rest incorrectly. For example, *as* instead of *so*, *saw* instead of *was*, *with* instead of *what*, *wistful* instead of *wise*, *icicles* instead of *ice crystals*. Such errors are made in almost every line. Careful re-examination showed no defect of vision.

To summarize the results on reading, I may say that the dull boys, as a group, are decidely inferior to the bright boys. They are less fluent, miscall more words, and have far less expression. The tone of voice is more monotonous and has more of the unnatural "schoolroom" pitch. The reading is evidently also by smaller units, phrases often being uttered separately as though unconnected. The frequently misplaced emphasis shows that fine shades of meaning are not grasped. Their rate is also decidedly slower, especially with *K*, *M*, and *N*. It must be kept in mind, however, that the stupid boys have done much less reading. (See Individual Sketches, Section XI below.) It cannot, of course, be determined how much of the difference is thus to be accounted for.

I believe that careful experimentation giving a detailed analysis of the reading process among these fourteen boys would have yielded important results. Even the mere verbal recognition of words involves the use of intricate mental machinery, and if there is a hitch at any part of it the process is seriously interfered with. Add to this more mechanical phase the accompanying interpretative processes necessary to good reading and we have opportunity for a wide range of mental ability to show itself.

In the first place, reading rate is a measure of the rate of association. Letters become associated together in certain combinations making words, words into word-groups and sentences. Recognition is for the most part an associative process. Rapid and accurate association will mean ready recognition of the printed forms. Since language units (whether letters, words, or word groups) have more or less preferred associations according to their habitual arrangement into larger units, it comes about that in the normal mind under normal conditions these preferred sequences arouse the apperceptive complex necessary to make a running recognition rapid and easy.   It is reasonable to suppose that in the sub-normal mind the habitual common associations are less firmly fixed, thus diminishing the effectiveness of the ever changing apperceptive expectancy. Reading is therefore largely dependent on what James calls the "fringe of consciousness" and the "consciousness of meaning."   In reading connected matter every unit is big with a mass of tendencies.   The smaller and more isolated the unit the greater is the number of possibilities.   Every added unit acts as a modifier limiting the number of tendencies until we have finally, in case of a large mental unit, a fairly manageable list.   When the most logical and suitable of these associations arise easily from subconsciousness to consciousness, recognition is made easy, and their doing so will depend on whether the habitual relations of the elements have left permanent traces in the mind.[1]

The reading of the sub-normal subject bears a close analogy to the reading of non-sense matter by the normal person.   It has been ascertained by experiment that such reading requires about twice as much time as the reading of connected matter. This is true for the reason that out of thousands of associations possible with each word, no particular association is favored. The apperceptive expectancy, practically *nil* in the reading of non-sense material, must be decidedly deficient in all poor reading.

With the ordinary reader, also, there is a feeling of rightness or wrongness about the thought sequences.   That my poorer subjects have this sense of fitness to a much less degree is evidenced by their passing over words so mutilated in pronunciation as to deprive them of all meaning.   The transposition of letters and words and the failure to observe marks of punctuation, point to the same thing.   In other words, all the reading of the stupid subject is (to him) with more or less non-sensical material.

2.   *Word making.*   Four trials were given, on different days, in constructing words out of given letters.   The first test was ten minutes in length and the letters were t e i a b r. Record was kept of the number of words made during each two-minute period.   The second test was the same with the letters m e k i a f g n.   The third lasted only eight minutes and a different set of letters was given for each two-minute period. They were (1) r n a d o, (2) o s d n a e, (3) c d o b u v e r,

---

[1] I am indebted for much in the above discussion of the intellectual processes of reading to Dr. E. B. Huey's paper on The Psychology and Physiology of Reading, *Am. Jour. of Psy.*, 1900.

(4) p y a h n t e.   The fourth was a similar test with the letters (1) k r e o p d a, (2) n t e s a i p, (3) b m o t a e k, (4) m o n e d i e.   The following is the ranking obtained from these four tests.

GROUP I.

A	B	C	D	E	F	G
3	1	6	5	9	6	4

GROUP II.

H	I	J	K	L	M	N
13	11	8	9	2	14	12

A good many factors enter into the success of this sort of work.   Much depends, of course, upon the vocabulary at command, and this in turn depends largely upon home training and amount of habitual reading as well as upon native retentiveness.   A second factor is ability to spell, and habits of word analysis generally.   Very important, also, is the use of a rational plan; some skipped about and made combinations at random, while others took the letters one by one and joined them in as many different ways as possible with the others. Lastly, the rate of shifting of attention, and the degree of mental inertia as opposed to spontaneity, also contribute to the total result.

Without going into details we may state that considering what the previous tests had revealed the results gained from this one are close to what one would have anticipated.   *E, H, I, J, K, M* and *N* show least plan of procedure, just as they did in the puzzle series.   The ones who are deficient in spelling, amount of reading done, ability to read, etc., also did poorly here.   Perhaps the only surprise is that *L* did so well, though his reading and general command of language would cause us to expect him to far outstrip the others of his group.

3.   *The Mutilated text.*   Two trials were made of the Ebbinghaus test (5).   1. The subjects were given the following mutilated story and were told to fill the blanks as they thought it ought to be done.

THE STRENGTH OF THE EAGLE.

One —— —— eagle —— with the —— birds —— see —— could—— —— highest.   —— agreed —— he who —— fly —— —— should—— called —— strongest ——.   All started —— —— same —— and —— away among —— cl——.   One by —— they —— weary —— re——, but —— eagle —— upward and —— un—— —— was—— mere speck —— —— heav——.   When he —— back —— others were —— for him; and —— —— touched —— —— a linnet —— off —— back where —— —— —— hidden and —— that —— himself —— —— strongest ——. "—— —— stronger —— —— ——," said the ——"for not —— did I—— as high but —— he began —— downward —— I — my hiding —— and —— up ——little ——."   —— this boastful —— the —— —— their heads and —— —— council to —— the matter. After —— long —— —— decided —— the —— —— the —— bird —— not only —— he —— so high, but —— —— the —— as well.

To —— day —— plumes —— —— —— are emblems of str—— and cour——

The results are summarized as follows:

TABLE V.

Test with mutilated text.

Grade.	Time.	Making sense.	Making non-sense.	Blanks not filled.	GENERAL REMARKS.
A	4	35	30	31	0	Much non-sense. Haphazard. Steady rate.
B	1	26	9	0	3	Almost all correct. All makes connected sense. Quick, steady, looks ahead.
C	2	15	12	7	8	Lazy, attention relaxed. Calculates time it will take to finish.
D	2	17	25	10	0	Some idea of meaning as whole. Got the main idea. Worked hard. Works to get meaning.
E	3	35	21	23	0	Phrases well connected. Little meaning to sentences as wholes. Lost main idea. Rather inattentive.
F	2	30	24	6	0	Attempts sense. Original. Misses main point. All makes fair sense. Looks ahead one or two sentences.
G	1	19	10	0	0	Nearly all correct. Runs through to get meaning and fills easiest first.
H	5	15	24	43	2	Rapid, careless, got none of the story. Works by phrases, No sentences.
I	5	25	37	32	0	Nearly all non-sense. *E. g.*, two verbs together. One word on two blanks and *vice versa*. No lack of confidence, no hesitation.
J	4	45	37	29	0	Fills it as a number of fragments. The sentences have no connection. Filled blanks steadily.
K	5	25	28	36	0	All non-sense except one or two easy parts, Phrases at a time. Confident. Little hesitation, steady.
L	3	35	6	6	25	Tries to make sense but omits much because he can't get the crucial sentences. Does well what he fills. Wants to quit because he can't understand it.

Making sense., Making non-sense., Blanks not filled.

TABLE V.—*Continued.*

| Grade. | Time. | Errors. | | | General Remarks. |
		Making sense.	Making non-sense.	Blanks not filled.	
M	5	40	8	2	61	All omitted but very easiest parts. Worked hard. Runs through all the story but can get no meaning.
N	3	14	12	7	27	Rather careful to avoid non-sense. Attention relaxed. Had to be encouraged.

The following gives an idea of the amount of difference between one of the best and one of the poorest.

B. One day an eagle went with the other birds to see who could fly the highest. They agreed that he who could fly the highest should be called the strongest bird. All started at the same time and flew away among the clouds. One by one they became weary and returned, but the eagle went upward and upward until he was a mere speck in the heavens. When he came back the others were waiting for him; and when he touched the ground a linnet flew off his back where the thief had hidden and said that he himself was the strongest bird. "I am stronger than you are" said the linnet, "for not alone did I fly as high, but as he began flying downward then I left my hiding place and flew up a little higher." But this boastful —— the —— —— their heads and went to council to decide the matter. After a long time they decided that the eagle was the strongest bird, and not only because he flew so high, but he had the strength as well. To this day the plumes of the eagle are emblems of strength and courage.

K. One with the eagle and with the small birds and see who could fly the highest, and agreed and he who will fly the higest should be called the strongest they All started in the same place and whent away among the clouds. One by one they were weary and returned, but the eagle flew upward and could less he was in mere speck and was heavy. When he came back the others were gone for him; and so he touched his wing a linnet and off whent back where he was then hidden and thought that he himself was the strongest I, "am the stronger and so he" said the brid, "for not and did I go as high but then he began to downward and I in my hiding place and whent up a little high." and this boastful in the way of their heads and had a council to take the matter. After a long while he decided that the king of the little bird and not only and he was so high, but he did the thing as well. To more day can plumes and so they are emblems of strait and course.

2. In order to rob the test of its puzzle nature a second trial was given with the following mutilated story; but in this case the complete story was read aloud to the subject first. He therefore knew the general sense and had a much narrower field to hunt over in the search for suitable words.

WHY THE MOLE IS BLIND.

An Indian once —— —— —— into cloud ——. Then —— —— ——

trap ——— ———, laughing to —— how —— would ——— ——— The ——
did ——— ——— back, but ———. The —— on —— daily ——— ———
right ——— ——— ———.

When —— bright ———— — ——— ——— come the —— began —— be ———,
and when ——— found his —— had ——— —— fast he ——— ——— know
——— ——— do.

He tried ——— ——— near enough —— —— the cords, but ——— ——— from
the ——— ——— him and he gave ——— ———.

Then ——— ——— many —— to try ———, but —— all found ——— ———
too ———. At —— the ——— ———, "I will —— through ——— ——— under
the —— and so get at ——— ———."

This —— ———, and the ——— ——— up —— —— h———.

But it —— so ——— that the poor ——— —— not ——— ———, and the ——
of ——— ——— ——— out his ———.

——— then the ——— have had ——— ——— ——— dark —— and unless
one —— very ——— he ——— ——— find ——— ———.

The following table summarizes the results:

TABLE VI.

Results of test with mutilated text.

| | Grade. | Time. | Errors. | | | GENERAL REMARKS. |
			Making sense.	Making non-sense.	Blanks not filled.	
A	2	25	30	7	2	All fair sense. Phrases now and then wrongly turned. Goes over it all and fills easiest first.
B	1	17	34	0	0	All good sense, but large changes made. Very careful with every blank.
C	1	9	18	0	0	All good sense. Only slightest changes. Whispers a good deal.
D	1	11	18	3	0	Nearly all makes sense. Much whispering. Works by fits and starts.
E	2	24	27	0	13	Fair sense but for the omissions. Several changes. Works steadily.
F	1	17	17	0	1	Good sense. Only very slightest changes. Worked steadily.
G	1	13	14	0	0	All the sense good. Only very slightest changes. Works through it as a whole.
H	5	15	19	56	5	Nearly all non-sense. Jumbled in all sorts of ways. Often two words in one blank. Very little hesitation.
I	4	30	39	31	10	Sense here and there, but great changes and much non-sense. Extra words inserted. Fills by phrases. Worked steadily.

TABLE VI.—*Continued.*

Grade.	Time,	Errors.			GENERAL REMARKS.
		Making sense.	Making non-sense.	Blanks not filled.	
J	3	25	28	8	16	Fairly good in almost half, rest poor. Some non-sense. A few extra words inserted. Fills by phrases. Worked very hard.
K	3	18	33	20	0	Much non-sense. Very many errors that change meaning. Extra words inserted. No hesitation.
L	2	30	36	0	8	Much better than others of this group. Many phrases turned but sense kept. Original in expression. Goes through to get sense.
M	5	30	30	3	47	Only about half filled, most of this wrong. Runs through it as a whole but can't get meaning.
N	3	25	24	4	14	Most of it makes sense but many phrases changed. Much whispering. Has to be encouraged.

Following are samples of the work of the two groups.

F. An Indian once chased a squirrel into cloudland. Then he set a trap for him, laughing to see how he would catch him. The squirrel did not come back, but—! The sun on his daily trip jumped right into the trap. When the bright sun did not come the Indian began to be frighten, and when he found his trap had the sun fast he did not know what to do. He tried to get near enough to losen the cords, but the heat from the sun scorched him and he gave it up. Then he got many animals to try it, but they all found the heat two great. At that the mole said, "I will dig through the ground under the trap and so get at the sun." This he done, and the sun went up to the heavens. But it went so fast that the poor mole could not get out, and the heat of the sun put out his eyes. So then the moles have had their homes in dark places and unless one looks very sharp he cannot find the mole.

H. An Indian once taued [chased] a squared [squirrel] into cloud after him. Then he sairtng [setting] that trap would catch him laughing to himself how would would he catch him. The squared did not come back, but sun The day on one daily the Indian right did not catch sun. When sun didnt bright Indian the he come sun began sun to be there, and when Indian found his trap had caut sun fast he did not know what to do.

He tried to gether near enough but tried the cords, but sun was from the hot and him and he gave it up. Then he again many time to try but he all found it was to heard [heat]. At then the Indian, "I will call through amigle [auimals] under the the and so get at the trap." This mole said, and the he get up then uned [under] hearth [earth.] But it he was so quik out that the poor mole could not get out well, and the ―――― of ――― ――― ――― out his ――――. But then the mole have had to live in the dark but and unless one come very quik he was found find blind mole.

The results of the two tests run closely parallel. With certain exceptions the two groups are widely separated in each. *A*, however, ranks below *L* in both tests and below *N* in the first. *E* is also rather poor. *H*, *I*, *J*, *K* and *M* stand far below all the others.

Ebbinghaus regards this test as a reliable measure of intellectual ability. The following is his description of that ability. "It does not depend upon knowing many things, *i. e.*, upon the reappearance in consciousness of definite individual impressions and on reacting to these with ideas one has already associated therewith. It is much more complex, more creative. Its essence lies in comprehending together in a unitary, meaningful whole, impressions which are independent of each other and answer to associations which are heterogeneous and partly contradictory. Intellectual ability consists in the elaboration of a whole into its worth and meaning by means of many-sided combination, correction, and completion of numerous kindred associations. . . . . It is a *combination* activity."

My experience with the test causes me to regard it favorably; but like all others, if taken alone it can only give a partial account of the subject's ability. It certainly does indicate something as to the general command of language. I am inclined to think that somewhat mechanical activities like memory and association, as distinguished from synthetic or combinative processes, play a relatively more important rôle in this test than Ebbinghaus assigns to them. Indeed, verbal memory, in the broad sense, would seem to be the chief factor in success. It gives what we term *fluency* in language. Verbal memory also means ability to carry the story as a whole, and therefore to see the connections in meaning running through it.

Something depends on the degree of acquaintance with this sort of literature, and perhaps still more upon peculiarities of language development in the subject. Greater originality and less imitation displayed by the subject in language acquisition will mean a poorer showing in this test, all else being equal. The method, also, of going about the task influences the final result to an important degree. The rational way is to look first over the entire story to get a conception of the whole. This was the method adopted by those who did best. In fact several of group II did not even rise to a conception of the fact that the text as a whole must make sense. These filled the blanks in just the order they were come upon and the result was either complete non-sense or else a series of phrases and clauses making fair sense within themselves but not connected with each other.

4. *Spelling.* Two lists of 50 words each were given to the

subjects on different days to be spelled.   I pronounced the
word, the subject writing it.   Misspelled words in the other
written exercises were also marked.   From all the data thus
obtained our subjects rank as follows, on a scale of five.

GROUP I.

A	B	C	D	E	F	G
2	1	2	3	3	1	1

GROUP II.

H	I	J	K	L	M	N
5	3	4	5	3	5	5

The reader may be inclined to have little regard for spelling
as a test for mental ability, on the ground that ability to spell
depends on the more :or less fortuitous formation of certain
restricted habits of observation and word analysis, habits not
so very essential to good speaking or reading.   There is no
doubt a certain amount of truth in this contention.   From
observation, however, I believe that this is more often true of
adults well on in life than of school children.   That is, adults
are likely to forget their spelling in proportion as their attention gravitates toward larger and more vital interests.   A well
known American scientist of undoubted genius confesses that
he has lost to a considerable degree his ability to spell common
English words.   His students readily perceive in him a similar
lack of attention to details of any sort that are regarded as
formal or trivial.   And yet this same man has an astonishing
command over detailed and curious information of other kinds,
especially of whatever happens to have significance for his
scientific theories.

As another instance, I am acquainted with a man who is recognized in his community as possessed of more than ordinary business ability.   As a youth he taught a country school, and I have
learned from reliable sources that in the old-fashioned spelling
matches he was noted for his ability to "stand the floor."   At
present he misspells all but the commonest words.   He has no
fixed way of writing a word, but employs any thinkable combination of letters that will represent the proper sound.   In
handling concepts of business import he has neglected the to
him trivial art of spelling and so has lost it, just as many an able
college president has forgotten his Latin or Greek paradigms.
Without disputing that intellectual ability is often more or less
one sided, I still seriously doubt whether there are many boys
and girls whom we can in any sense regard as extraordinarily
intelligent who with honest application could not learn to spell
tolerably well.   With regard to my subjects, I believe the

differences in their ability to spell are significant. Unlike the scientist and business man mentioned above, they have been compelled in their daily school work to pay heed to their spelling, and this is true to approximately the same degree of all the subjects. Moreover, they have not yet reached the age when abstractions have replaced formal observation, when microscopic vision has become telescopic.

5. *Power of Expression.* It is rather difficult to state clearly what is included under this term and yet the idea is fairly definite. The grading was done very much as one would grade ordinary school compositions, except that nothing was allowed for penmanship, neatness, spelling, punctuation, etc. Among other factors are fluency, coherency, richness of vocabulary, spontaneity and readiness of speech, correctness of grammatical construction, sentence structure, directness or awkwardness of expression, etc. With such a variety of items contributing to the total result, the grading can be nothing more than approximate. It is valuable, however, as indicating the exceptional subjects.

After a great deal of careful consideration both of their conversational language and of the written work which they did in other tests I arrived at the following grades. It is to be regretted that data were not secured such as would have made it possible for this ranking to be made by several others besides myself. The same is true of some of the other rankings.

GROUP I.

A	B	C	D	E	F	G
2	1	1	2	4	2	1

GROUP II.

H	I	J	K	L	M	N
5	3	3	4	2	3	3

The two most striking facts are the low position of E and the relatively high position of L; H is also lower than in the previous tests.

I have tried to characterize in a word or two the salient points for each subject. *A.* Fluent, wordy, awkward turns in expression, well connected. *B.* Clear, logical, coherent, words well chosen, beautiful style. *C.* Very fluent, bookish tone, rather flamboyant. *D.* Fair, but not striking. *E.* Sentences run together by *ands*, many words omitted, very incoherent and broken, hazy in meaning. *F.* Clear, brief, to the point. *G.* Logical, exact, careful. *H.* Hazy, indefinite, sentences connected by *ands*, many omissions of words, parts sound like non-sense phrases strung together. *I.* Fairly good, nothing striking. *J.* Separate sentences fairly good, but they do not follow one another naturally, a certain stiffness. *K.* Awkward, many *ands.* *L.* Fluent, marked tendency to use of big words, plainly ahead of his group in power of expression. *M.* Stiff and forced style, lacks fluency. *N.* A certain glibness, but childish in his manner of expression and in the frequent repetitions.

6. *Execution of commands.* A good indication of one's mastery of language is the ability to understand and carry out complicated verbal directions. It is commonly recognized as a sign of stupidity for one to blunder in trying to execute simple commands. A child can seldom be depended on to do a thing according to instructions, however unequivocal, apparently, the instructions may be. For the undeveloped mind such directions are little more than a jumbled mass of familiar sounds, the separate parts probably arousing the appropriate images, but the whole not comprehended in its logical significance.

To test this sort of language mastery thirty separate commands were given, orally, for moving chess men on a chess board.

The following are examples of the commands:
1. White.   Move the king's pawn two steps.
2. Black.   The same.
3. White.   Move the king's bishop to his queen's bishop's fourth square.
4. Black.   The same.
5. White.   Move the queen's bishop's pawn one step.
6. Black.   Move the queen's knight to his bishop's third square, etc.

This test was given after the chess practice to be described below (Section VIII) and none of the directions involved any points that the subjects were not familiar with. Important differences came out. The subjects of group I, as a rule, went to work to execute the command without question or much hesitation, while those of group II on hearing the command frequently looked up with blank face and some such expression as "What do you mean?" "I don't know what you want me to do!" "Show me," etc. The table gives the chief results.

TABLE VII.

Execution of commands.

Rank	Average time in seconds per move.	Number of errors.	REMARKS.
A	3	11	8	Corrected all his errors. Five moves under one second.

TABLE VII.—*Continued.*

	Rank	Average time in seconds per move.	Number of errors.	REMARKS.
B	1	5	2	All but two of his moves under eight seconds. Very little difficulty. Nine moves under one second.
C	2	4	7	Very quick, impulsive, some of his errors evidently due to this.
D	3	6	10	Repeats the instructions in a whisper, moves quickly, later corrects, six under one second.
E	2	6	8	Eight under one second. Had to be showed one move.
F	4	12	11	Failed on four moves, five under one second.
G	2	6	6	Very little difficulty. Eight under one second.
H	5	13	20	Asked that several commands be repeated. Failed on five, five under one second.
I	5	16	15	Asked several repetitions, failed on four, one under one second.
J	4	13	15	Two repetitions, three failures, four under one second.
K	5	14	17	Five failures, one repetition, one under one second.
L	3	12	18	Two failures. Those he can understand at all he executes at once. Two repetitions, seven under one second.
M	5	21	17	Six failures, two under one second. Whispers over directions two or three times slowly.
N	4	11	13	Asked repetition four times. Three failures, one under one second, most of moves quickly made.

The table on page 352 gives the grades for all of the language tests.

VII. INTERPRETATION OF FABLES.

E. J. Swift (20) suggests that a subject's reaction to a complex situation is a better test of his intelligence than are the methods usually employed. Dr. Swift proposed three "situations" and the pupils of several schoolrooms were allowed to write what they thought of each: 1st, concerning the boy who put his hand into a jar to take out some nuts and grasped so many that he could not withdraw his hand. 2nd, the story of the soldier who in time of peace neglected to care for the horse that in war had served him faithfully. On the return of

TABLE VIII.

Grades and Ranking based on the Mastery of Language.

	Reading.	Word making.	Eagle Blanks.	Mole Blanks.	Spelling.	Expression.	Execution of oral commands.	Composite Ranking.
A	2	2	4	2	2	2	3	6
B	1	1	1	1	1	1	1	1
C	1	3	2	1	2	1	2	3
D	2	3	2	1	2	2	3	4
E	3	4	3	2	3	4	2	8
F	2	3	2	1	1	2	4	4
G	1	2	1	1	1	1	2	2
H	4	5	5	5	5	5	5	14
I	3	4	5	4	3	3	5	10
J	4	4	4	3	4	3	4	9
K	4	4	5	3	5	4	5	12
L	3	1	3	2	3	2	3	6
M	4	5	5	5	5	3	5	13
N	5	4	3	3	5	3	4	10

war the famished horse gave way under the weight of his rider. 3rd, Pestalozzi's fable of the Fish and the Pike. The fish were being eaten by the pike and brought suit against the latter. The judge, a pike, decided that he would mend matters by allowing two fish to become pike every day.

A comparison was made by Dr. Swift between the papers of his "brightest" and "dullest" subjects, with the result that he found no superiority on either side.

In order to give a further trial to this sort of test I allowed my subjects to give their interpretation to twelve fables which I selected after examining several hundred. I took each subject alone, read to him a fable, and then asked him to state orally what he thought it meant. The answers were therefore spontaneous and lacked the stilted and unnatural tone so common in the written exercises of the school. I cannot take space to repeat the fables here in full, but the substance of each is given below:

1. The fate of the stork which was caught in a trap set for cranes and was compelled to die along with the cranes. 2. The monkey that by use of flattery coaxed the cat to rake the master's chestnuts from the hot ashes. 3. The wolf that hired a crane to relieve him of a bone fast in his throat. After the work was done the wolf refused the promised pay and said that the crane had been paid by not having his head bitten off. 4. The girl who carried her milk to market and while calculating the eggs she could buy, the chicks she could produce from them, etc., tossed her head proudly and let fall the milk.

5. The camel that begged his master for room in the tent and then forced his master out. 6. The miller and his son who took their ass to town to sell. They walked, rode, or carried him just as people suggested until finally the animal fell into the river. 7. The foolish sheep who, at the request of the wolves, sent away the dogs that guarded them and so fell prey to their enemies. 8. The dispute between the wind and the sun as to who was the stronger. They decided by seeing which one could first make the traveller remove his coat. 9. The tortoise that begged the eagle to teach her to fly. The eagle bore her aloft and let her fall to earth. 10. The jackdaw that painted himself white and tried to live with the doves. After expulsion from their company his own mates refused to take him in. 11. The frog who tied the mouse to his leg by a string and then jumped into the water. As the drowned mouse floated on the surface it was seized by a hawk, who carried it away together with the frog and devoured both. 12. The maids who killed the cock which woke their mistress so early. No longer able to tell the time of night the mistress aroused her maids earlier than ever.

Finally, in order to secure results that could be compared to Dr. Swift's, I proposed to my subjects the same three stories that he used. We have therefore fifteen separate tests of this sort; a number sufficient to carry us beyond accidental variations in the quality of the answers. A subject will now or then do better or worse than we expect, but on the whole his level of efficiency in this kind of work can be estimated with a good deal of accuracy from a sufficient number of trials. The following are examples of the replies precisely as given by word of mouth, except for a few abbreviations. A casual glance will reveal significant and characteristic differences between the two groups. The poorest answers are italicised.

The Storks and the Cranes. A. To beware of taking other people's property. *B.* To think out what we do before we do it. *C.* That if you are caught with wrong things, they'll do the same with you as if you were bad. *D.* It means that if he was caught with them, he would have to die with them. *E.* Teaches us to keep away from bad company. *F.* Teaches us not to be caught with bad people. *G.* One is just as bad as the other if they steal. Don't know what it teaches. *H. Lesson is that it learns us to catch cranes and storks. I. It teaches us how to catch birds. J. Teaches us that cranes eat corn. K.* It means that — the cranes not to come and eat the grain again, and they lose their life for a little bit of grain. *L.* Don't know. *M. Not to go in those traps. N.* Teaches not to be with the birds that took the stuff.

The girl and her milk. A. Teaches us not to be too proud and not to say anything before you do it. *B.* Not to plan ahead too far. *C.* Not to make your plans until you've got something to make them with, and don't be too sure that they will work. *D.* She was too proud. She ought not to have counted her chickens before they were hatched. *E.* Not to count your chickens before they are hatched. *F.* She felt proud. Teaches us not to be too proud. *G.* Don't count your chickens before they are hatched. *H.* Learns her a lesson not to talk about anything before she gets it, and *not to carry a pail on her head. I. To not be too gay when you have anything, you might lose it. J.* Not to be too proud. When you be proud why everything goes back on you. *K*. Warns you not to be too proud. She thought that she was going to get so much and she got left. *L*. Not to be too proud. *M. Not to think we are so big. N*. Same as that she had n't ought to count her chickens before they were hatched.

The Arab and his camel. A. Not to let people do too much or they might do the same as the camel did. *B*. Don't know. The Arab ought not have let the camel in at all. *C*. When you get small things, don't ask for big things and don't put everybody else out. *D*. It was a greedy camel and teaches that the Arab had n't ought to let him in. *E*. The Arab knew that the camel was big and the tent was small. He ought to just let him put his head and neck in. *F*. Teaches us not to divide too much. *G*. Teaches us not be too good to selfish people. *H. Learns a lesson to the Arab not to stay in his tent with the camel again. I. To give poor people things and not the rich.* (Why?) Because he let the camel in and got out himself. *J*. Not to let anybody in when you think the place too small. *K*. Teaches the man not to let anything into his house again. He will get put out instead of the camel. *L. The camel thought he'd make the Arab go out there too as long as he kept his poor camel out. The camel was foxier than what he was. M*. Not to be selfish. The camel was selfish and wanted all the tent. *N*. That the Arab had n't ought to a been so foolish. Had n't ought to a let the camel have so much room.

The Miller, his boy and the ass. A. To care for others, not for yourself. The farmer did n't care for himself, he cared for his boy and ass. *B*. Not to pay any attention to other people. *C*. That if you try to please everybody, you won't please anybody and you will get into trouble yourself. *D*. They tried to please everybody and pleased nobody. *E*. That they had n't ought to mind every one. *F*. Teaches us not to try to please other people. *G*. Don't take everybody's advice. *H. Learns them a lesson not to carry a donkey across the bridge, or carry them any place. I. It means to help the old people instead of the young. J. Not to try to carry anything that is too heavy—A thing that kicks and everything. K*. Teaches the man not to mind what anybody else says. *L*. They thought they would sell the donkey, and before they got there the donkey fell into the river. *It teaches us not to think it till we are sure. M*. The miller wanted to do just as people told him to do. (Ought we?) Not always. *N*. They tried to please everybody and could not please themselves.

The Jackdaw and the doves. A. It means not to try to get into another company when you belong to one, or you might miss both. *B*. We should be contented with what we are. *C*. When you are one thing don't try to be something else. *D*. That the Jackdaw ought to have been contented with what he had. *E*. He was too proud of himself. He wanted to cut out every one else, and got caught. *F*. Not to try to look like others. *G*. You must not try to get what does not belong to you. *H. Learns us a lesson not to paint ourselves white and try to go into some other family. I*. Not to try to get into other company. *J. Not to do anything, paint yourself or anything, if you ain't a dove, or else you will never get back.* *K*. The Jackdaw wanted too much. It teaches him not to go to anybody else's place to get food. *L. That if he wanted to belong to the dove cote he ought to a kept still.* He wanted to belong to both companies, but by being a little bit fresh he could n't. *M*. Not to try to do what you can't do. *N*. Not to try to be somebody else. He ought to have lived the way he was always living.

The frog and the mouse. A. Not to be unkind or you'll get into trouble. *B*. To show kindness to our neighbors. *C*. Shows how foolish the mouse was to try to do something she knew she could not. *D*. The frog had so much pride and thought he'd harm the mouse, and after he did he got harmed more. *E*. Teaches not to be too kind like the mouse was. *F*. Teaches you not to be unkind to people. *G*. To do to others as they have done to you, because the mouse had showed him everything and did not hurt him. *H*. Learns a lesson to the mouse not to go in the water for he can't swim; *and learns the frog not to tie a piece of grass to his leg and the mouse's leg. I*. Not to take anybody else in a bad place. *J*. *Teaches you not to go if you think you can't swim. K*. (Omitted by mistake.) *L*. Teaches us not to be silly like the frog. *M*. Not to be foolish. *N*. The mouse was foolish. He might know he would get drowned if he went in the water.

The maids and the cock. A. Not to work your children too hard. B. That we ought not to try to disarrange any one else's plans. *C*. That the little maidens had not ought to a killed the cock without their mother's advice. *D*. Teaches that they ought to have left the cock alone and they would have been all right. *E*. Teaches us not to do anything wrong. *F*. Not to do wrong. *G*. Don't know. *H*. Learns a lesson not to kill a cock when he wakes them up early in the morning and so they can't tell what time it is. *Teaches us not to kill a cock. I. Not to give any little person any hard work. J. Not to kill anything else you'll get woke up just the same. K*. (Omitted by mistake.) *L*. Not to be so silly like the maids and kill the cock, for the cock was not to blame. *M*. Teaches the girls not to be lazy. *N*. That they ought to have been satisfied with getting up when the cock crowed instead of getting up in the middle of the night.

The fishes and the pike. A. I think the judge ought to a done something to the pike. (Fair?) No.—Fair in one way though, to let the little fish become pike, but he ought to a punished the pike. *B*. Not fair. (Why?) Because the more pike there became, the faster they would eat the little fish. *C. It might be better for the little fish in some ways,—they would not be eaten up*. It would be bad for the pikes because they would have nothing to eat. *D*. That was all right, but then if only two are changed to pike the others would get eaten up. *E*. While the two fish are changing into pike the rest of the little fish would get eaten up by them. *F*. (Omitted by mistake.) *G*. It was all right, but it was kind of funny that they didn't do anything to the pike. *H*. It will learn the little fish to keep away from the pikes. (Good or bad decision?) *Bad cause they were gittin turned into pikes. I. Good decision, because the little fish was turning into big ones and the big fish wouldn't dare to eat them now. J. The judge was kind enough to let them be a pike. K. He ought to let all the fish be pike if he was going to let two, cause the other little fish was as good as the two. L. Fair decision, for two would be turned to pike every day and not be eaten up. M*. If the pike could eat up all the little ones in a day it would not be a good decision. *N*. Don't know. He ought to a stopped the pike from eating up the little fishes.

Group II show two chief points of inferiority. In the first place, they more frequently miss the point of the story altogether. For example, *H* and *I* think that fable 1 teaches us how to catch birds. *J* thinks it teaches that cranes eat corn. In 5, *I* thought the Arab got out of the tent of his own accord as an act of charity. *H* and *J* interpreted fable 6 as a warning against carrying a donkey or *anything else that kicks! I* thinks it teaches respect for old age. In answer to 15, *H* thought it was bad for the little fish to be turned into pike. *I, J,* and *L* thought it was very kind of the judge to change them into pike. From such replies it is evident that, as a whole, group II are unable to appreciate fine shades of meaning. They know in a general way what is being talked about, but they fail to comprehend much that to us seems clearly expressed. In fables, moreover, a good deal is frequently left to be inferred by the reader, and here always the dull subject is at a disadvantage. He cannot supply the meanings hinted at because he is insensible to the thought fringes. It is these that must give meaning to the fable; the dullest subject is apparently able to image the objects and activities described, but taken in the rough such imagery gets him no whither. They are like pieces of scrap iron that need welding to be of value.

In the second place the dull boys are plainly deficient in degree of abstraction. Even when they give an approximately correct interpretation they usually express it in the concrete terms of the given situation, instead of generalizing it. For example, *H* thinks fable 5 "learns the Arab not to stay in his tent with the camel again." In 10, *H* answers "learns us a lesson not to paint ourselves white and try to go into some other family." *J* "not to do anything, paint yourself white or anything, if you aint a dove, or else you will never get back." In 11, *H* sees only a warning to the frog never again to fasten a mouse's leg to his own with a piece of grass. *K* answers 14 thus: "It teaches the man when he has a horse to keep it and use it well." *M*, "the soldier ought to have fed him just the same when he didn't go to war." *L* replies to 2, "Its just like if you was stealing apples, and you steal them and another fellow eats them." 9, *H* "learns the tortoise not to fly when he ain't got any wings."

The better subjects answer nearly always in general terms and *N* of the stupid group did also, probably because of his advantage in age.

This last suggests that what is tested by the interpetation of fables is in part at least that general change of mental horizon that comes with increased experience and dawning maturity. But as mental deficiency is itself in many respects a sort of continued infantilism, this is, perhaps, not so much a point of criticism as of commendation.

My results with this test show such clear differences between the bright and dull groups that I cannot but think the method employed by Dr. Swift in making his tests somewhere at fault. I should judge that his results would have been different if he had been able to take his cases individually instead of collectively.

The grades as I have estimated them for the tests with the fables are given in the following table.

TABLE IX.
Grades and Ranking based on the Interpretation of Fables.

Fables.	1	2	3	4	5	6	7	8	9	10	11	12	13	14	15	Rank.
A	4	4	2	3	1	5	4	4	5	2	2	2	1	3	4	8
B	4	3	3		3	1	2	4	1	1	2	2	1	3	1	1
C	1	2	3	1	2	1	4	5	1	1	2	4	1	3	5	2
D	2	4	4	2	3	1	3	4	4	1	4	4	2	4	3	6
E	1	4	2	1	1	1	5	4	4	4	4	2	1	3	2	4
F	1	4	5	4	1	1	4		4	2	3	2		3	2	6
G	4	2		1	1	1	1	4	1	3	3		2	3	2	3
H	5	5	5	4	4	5	4	5	4	3	4	5	4	5	5	14
I	5	5	5	4	5	5	5	4	1	1	4	4	1	4	5	9
J	5	4	2	4	3	5	4	4	4	5	5		1	5	5	11
K	5	4	4	4	4	1	4	5	4	5			2	4	3	10
L		3	5	4	5	5	4		2	5		4	1	4	5	13
M	5		4	4	3	2	4		5	5	3	5	1	5	3	10
N	1	1	2	1	3	1	3	4	3	1	4	4	3	5	3	5

VIII. LEARNING TO PLAY CHESS.

A complex game, such as chess or checkers, undoubtedly makes extensive demands on intelligence. This statement is not contradicted by the fact that many expert players have accomplished little in the useful arts or sciences. They have probably lacked certain emotional and volitional qualities, making it impossible for them to apply their intellectual powers to other work. For example, it is obvious that the constructive imagination necessary for chess plays also a part in the success of the military strategist, while the moral and volitional qualities may be much more dissimilar. It is more likely the rarity of a suitable combination of the latter that accounts for the fewness of great military strategists, rather than the rarity of sufficient intellectual ability.

I intended to use checker-playing as a test, but finding that several knew something of the game, I gave chess instead. For three weeks, or about eight to ten hours in all, the subjects played in pairs, the bright against the dull. I watched the game and took extensive notes but did not record the separate moves. My judgment is, therefore, somewhat subjective, but the main differences are so evident that one could hardly mistake them.

The following table gives the chief facts. By "error" is meant moving a piece in some other way than is allowed by the rules. Ability to plan is graded on a scale of five. It should be explained that before beginning the playing I demonstrated all the main points of the game and also all the possible moves of each piece. This was repeated twice and the subject's questions were answered.

TABLE X.

Grading on Learning to Play Chess.

	Errors in 1st 100 moves.	Errors in 2nd 100 moves.	Rank on errors.	Grade on ability to plan.	GENERAL.
A	13	5	6	3	Several errors, poor defense, follows up a plan to neglect of rest of board, many "give-aways," quick.
B	2	0	1	1	Almost total absence of errors, by far the best player in all respects, never moves blindly, quick to grasp the situation and move.
C	1	2	2	2	Very few errors, effective planning, intermittent attention, and numerous motor automatisms. Nervously quick.
D	5	1	3	3	Few errors, occasional tendency toward aboulia, lack of sustained attention, and little plan, generally quick.
E	19	5	7	3	Relatively numerous errors, lack of sustained attention, general ineffectiveness due to a happy-go-lucky way of moving, quick.
F	7	1	5	3	Few errors, not very steady attention, short sighted, but deals fairly well with the immediate situation, quick.
G	7	0	4	2	Few errors, general ability to plan good attention, and quickness.
H	26	14	11	3	Many errors, readiness to capture and to defend pieces from immediate danger, ability to plan good as compared to errors, attentive, fairly quick. Has played checkers.
I	16	10	8	4	Numerous errors, overlooks capture, many "give-aways," general lack of plan, apparently attentive, fairly quick.
J	28	11	10	4	Numerous errors, vagueness of plan, inability to attend to more than one part of the board at once, absent-minded, fairly quick.
K	28	20	12	5	Many errors, many "give-aways," and general lack of plan. Slow.
L	23	15	9	4	Many errors, little plan, many "give-aways," good attention. Slow.
M	29	21	13	5	Very numerous errors, complete lack of offensive, over cautious, good attention, extremely slow, poorest player.
N	38	27	14	4	Frequent errors continued to the last. General lack of plan, attention not very steady, overlooks captures, many "give-aways." Slow.

A. Errors rather numerous at first but gradually eliminated. Played 16 games with *H* and won 6. Moves rapidly; median time about 3 seconds. Talks much about the progress of the game. Personifies the pieces. Plans ahead but neglects defense. Continually moves out pawns unsupported. Captures without noting result. The following notes, taken in 12th game, are typical: gives pawn to pawn; exposes bishop to castle, tries to trade knight for bishop; gives pawn to pawn; castle to pawn; bishop to queen; and queen to pawn.

B. No error after first game. Won 14 out of 15 with *L*, and 1 out of 2 with *C*. Median time per move less than 2 seconds. Showed curiosity about the rules and the purpose of the game. Seldom overlooks capture, not a move made blindly, laughs over the effect of bad moves, often asks whether I see his plan, guards king well, almost no "giveaways," usually wins from *L* with loss of only 2 or 3 pieces, talks to me while opponent studies his move. Not to be compared with any other players except *G* and *C*, and is far better than they are.

C. Very few errors. Won all of 12 games with *K*, and 1 of 2 with *B*. Nervously quick in moving. Median time less than 2 seconds. Does not attend to his plays half the time. Often stops to explain the outcome of different possible moves. Second only to *B*. Always plans ahead. Overlooks almost no captures. Has good ideas about the relative value of pieces. His showing injured by occasional inattention. Many motor automatisms while playing. (See section XI, below.)

D. Few errors. Won all of 12 games with *M*. Generally moves very quickly, but occasionally studies 5 to 10 minutes. On such occasions shows a tendency toward *aboulia* in his inability to decide what move to make. Fingers his pieces about, retracts moves, argues the advantages of different possible moves, and is unable to decide between alternatives. It does no good for me to hurry him; he wants to move quickly, but simply cannot. Perhaps his most striking trait is lack of sustained attention. Attends to other things while his opponent is moving. At his turn he gives a quick glance at the board and unless under a spell of *aboulia* moves without delay. Even when unable to move for several minutes, he does not study the board a third of the time. He touches different pieces, discusses moves, then talks of something, or even gets up and walks about, all the time keeping up a series of indescribable automatisms. Overlooks few captures, but shows little plan; overguards king and uses only a few pieces for the offense.

E. Worst of bright group on errors, but gradually left them off. Won 13 out of 17 games with *J*, and 2 out of 5 with *F*. Moves quickly, generally in less than 2 seconds. Seems careless and inattentive, as in all his work. Studies the board less than half the time. Sometimes, however, devotes a few seconds to working out an effective plan. Talks much about the plays. Quick to accept captures, but shows little initiative. Rather numerous "give-aways."

F. Few errors and these soon left off. Won three games out of 5 with *E* and 12 out of 14 with *I*. Moves rapidly at first, later is more cautious. Talks much about the progress of the game, but really studies the board very little. Looks about and talks with me. Lacks definite plan, but handles the immediate situation to fairly good advantage. Few "give-aways," accepts captures and makes use of all his pieces.

G. Very few errors. Won 16 out of 17 games with his older brother, *N*. Few moves take more than two seconds. Attentive, likes the game. Always plans ahead, seldom overlooks captures, few "give-aways." At first, overguards king, but later corrects the fault. Soon learns to take advantage of the fact that his opponent overlooks many captures, and so in order to locate his pieces where he wants them he exposes them to attack.   Regularly makes use of all the pieces.

H.   Many more errors than the poorest of the bright group.   The knight, bishop, and castle were wrongly moved to the last.   Won 10 out of 16 games with *A*.   Moves rapidly, seldom overlooks captures, few give-aways, good deal of plan.   Overguards the king, using only bishop and castle for attacking.   Makes captures to neglect of the real end of the game.   His rank on plan is rather surprising, considering his many errors.   This probably due to his having played checkers a greal deal.

I.   Many errors.   All the pieces wrongly moved to the last, but knight the worst offender.   Won 2 out of 14 games with *F*.   Extremely little plan; avoids only slightest difficulties; overlooks about half his opportunities to capture; overguards king; little conception of the relative value of the pieces; makes no use of his knight nor does he defend himself from his opponent's knight.   For example, in the 12th game, gives pawn to pawn, bishop to pawn, pawn to pawn, fails to take bishop with pawn, queen with queen, and overlooks the fact that his opponent's king is in check.   After being beaten several times he came to dislike the game.

J.   Made errors with all the pieces to the last game.   Won 4 out of 17 with *E*.   Moved quickly, except now and then when listless or absent-minded.   Sometimes forgot his turn to move.   Makes plans but cannot execute them.   Exposes his pieces to capture while working out a scheme.   Never moves knight without hesitating and counting spots.   In last game exposes knight to pawn, bishop to castle, castle to knight, castle to bishop, fails to take pawn with pawn, gives pawn to pawn, and captures his own piece.   Fights mostly with a bishop and castle.

K.   Many errors, pretty evenly scattered among the pieces.   Lost all of 12 games to *C*.   Moves slowly; little plan; captures without looking to the result; many "give-aways."   For example, in the 10th game, trades castle for pawn, moves up pawn alone and loses it, gives castle to pawn, pawn to pawn, knight to castle, pawn to pawn and trades bishop for pawn.

L.   A majority of the errors due to confusing the bishop and castle.   Out of 15 games with *B*, lost all but 1.   Deliberate, sometimes studying a move for two or three minutes.   Watches the board intently and says nothing during the game.   Little plan.   Habitually runs a pawn clear across the board alone to be captured.   Three times moves king out toward the centre of the board alone.   Gives many pieces away, but seldom fails to take captures offered.   In game 13, gives pawn to pawn, castle to pawn, pawn to pawn, knight to pawn, trades queen for bishop, fails to take bishop with knight, exposes castle to pawn, and king to pawn.   Knight little used, and the bishop and castle so confused as to be nearly worthless.

M.   Worst subject on errors.   No piece was fully learned.   Won none out of 12 games with *D*.   Exasperatingly slow.   Median time about 1½ minutes, and often studied a move 5 minutes.   Very attentive, never looking up except to ask how to move a piece.   Foresees only the immediate result of his moves.   Accomplishes nothing in attack.   Devotes all his attention to preventing loss of pieces.   Bunches nearly all around the king and moves back and forth with only one piece.

N Never sure of the move of any piece.   In last two games, makes the following errors: Moves pawn angularly twice; captures with pawn by moving straight forward; moves knight wrongly seven times;

castle forgotten three times; king too far once; four times makes turns with other pieces than the knight; and castles wrongly. These worse than some of the preceding games, probably because of decreasing interest. Rather slow. Lost 16 of 17 games with his younger brother, G. Avoids some losses, but little plan; a vague idea of what to do, but no definite idea of how to carry it out. Many "give-aways," often losing an important piece to a pawn. More intent on accepting pieces offered him than on creating new situations. Did not guard king till told by opponent to do so. On being checkmated is usually surprised and asks how it was done.

With regard to chess as a test of intelligence I may say that it clearly differentiates the two groups, and that so many interesting things came out that I regret not having had more time to devote to it. I should like the opportunity to choose two or three pairs of my subjects and observe them daily in chess or checkers for several months. I believe that the insight gained would amply repay the time expended.

IX. MEMORY.

Memory tests have been in the past rather unsatisfactory. It is practically impossible to get at the pure physiological retentiveness, while if we aim at testing the everyday working memory our results are still more disturbed by interests and habits of apperception. Memory in any case, considered as pure physiological retentiveness, would seem to be of no more than intermediate importance in a study of intellectual differences; more significant than sense differences but less so than the logical and creative processes. The great minds have more often had logical than desultory memories. There must of course be a certain minimum of physiological memory, as distinguished from the apperceptual, in order to make possible a distinctively human intelligence, but above this minimum limit we may have almost all grades of intellectuality according to the manner in which the atoms of experience are united by interest, association and meaning. A desultory memory can give us only the crude materials for genius. It is not till these fragments have lost their separate identity by coalescence into a whole,—by assuming a net-work of relations to one another—that intelligence emerges. So many different lines, of such varying degrees of importance, are open to habits of apperception that with a given amount of plasticity many grades of intelligence are possible. It may give us on the one hand an ignorant hotel attendant, with a memory that enables him to return to each of a hundred guests his own hat, or, on the other hand, a Humboldt, with a tenacious memory for the facts of science but unable (according to his own confession) to quote *verbatim* a single line of literature, either poetry or prose. It is mostly the character of the synthetic operations, combined with emotional and volitional qualities, that distinguishes the two minds. This is little more than to say that memory for the most part is particular rather than general, though there are a few minds that are encyclopædic and retain with little discrimination. For these and other reasons I do not regard my memory tests as of so very great importance. They are as follows:

1. Ability to reproduce a complex geometrical diagram. For this purpose I employed the diagram used by Binet in his own experiments on memory. The purpose of the experiment was explained to the subject and after one minute's exposure of the figure he was allowed to reproduce it, erasing and redrawing until satisfied.

2. Chess moves; see grading on errors, Table X above.

3. Reproduction in writing of a story heard. The story used was about 300 words long. This was a group experiment.

4. Same with another story about twice as long.

5. Oral reproduction of a story read. The subject was given five minutes in which to read and study the selection and then give it orally while I took down his words. This plan was followed to avoid the disinclination that some of the subjects seemed to have for writing. Greater spontaneity was also secured. The story was an interesting Indian legend about 200 words long.

6. Same with another story of about 500 words.

7. Ability to repeat the solution of a simple mechanical puzzle after watching its performance by another. The puzzle consisted of two iron links so made that they could be separated only by being turned in a certain way. My method was to hold the puzzle before the eyes of the subject and after soliciting his attention perform the separation myself slowly by three successive stages. He was urged to look closely and to remember the positions of the pieces in each stage of the solution. If he was then not able to make the separation himself within one minute I showed him again, and so on until the trick was perfectly learned. It is evident that after the first success the memory is partly a motor one, and even previous to such success the visual images may be retained partly through motor associations.

The following table shows the grading for each memory test on a scale of five. The mechanical puzzle gives results at so great variance with the other tests that I have not included it in making the composite ranking.

TABLE XI.
Grading and Ranking on Memory Tests.

	Binet's figure.	Chess moves.	First story heard.	Second story heard.	First story read.	Second story read.	Mechanical puzzle.	Composite ranking on memory
A	4	3	3	3	4	3	3	6
B	3	1	1	2	1	2	2	3
C	2	1	2	2	1	1	1	2
D	2	2	3	3	2	3	5	4
E	3	3	4	4	4	5	5	10
F	5	2	3	2	2	3	1	5
G	1	2	1	1	1	2	3	1
H	5	4	5	5	4	4	1	14
I	4	3	5	5	3	5	2	13
J	5	4	4	4	3	4	3	11
K	3	4	5	4	3	3	2	9
L	4	4	2	3	3	4	2	6
M	3	5	3	4	5	4		11
N	5	5	4	2	3	2	4	8

CHAPTER X. MOTOR ABILITY.

The theory that all mental traits tend to express themselves physically has long been held in one form or another. The moralist has always been reluctant to credit one with the possession of ethical qualities which never give direction to behavior, while recent psychology, with its experiments on muscle reading and its automatographic tracings, teaches that every idea is motor. Neurologists believe that motor activities have a reflex effect on all the functioning of the brain, and the salutary effects of manual training on intelligence give a basis for the theory. Bolton believes that the ability to take on new motor habits represents educability, and that the motor practice curve furnishes a reliable test of mental weakness. (2). Several attempts have been made to correlate intelligence with motor accuracy, rapidity, strength, etc., but with contradictory results. Kirkpatrick finds a positive correlation. Bagley a negative one. Havelock Ellis finds that British men of genius often show marked awkwardness of bodily control. Gesell finds a direct relation between mental ability as judged by the teacher and skill in handwriting. My own subjects are too few and my motor tests not adapted to the working out of mathematical correlations.

1. *The practice curve.* This was the most important motor test tried. The apparatus was a small wooden cup about two inches in diameter set on a wooden handle eight inches long.

At the middle of the handle was attached a string two feet in length, and to the end of the string was a wooden ball of the proper size to fit easily into the cup. The subject grasped the handle, gave the ball a swing upward and tried to catch it in the cup as it fell. Several elements enter into the success. 1. It is a test of visual-motor co-ordination. 2. Much depends upon motor memory, which in turn involves sense discrimination in the field of the "muscle" sense. 3. The higher processes are involved, inasmuch as there are certain points of method to be learned which make the catch much more certain. 4. Attention.

Each subject was given 40 trials with each hand at each visit to the laboratory until 2,000 trials were made, 1,000 for each hand. The method employed was to give 20 with the right hand, then 20 with the left, etc. The visits to the laboratory were not entirely regular, but for the most part were made every other day. The results were reckoned upon the following basis: A catch was scored as 0. If the ball dropped into the cup, but in such a way as to bound out again, the score 1 was given. If the ball simply struck the cup on the side or rim but did not drop in, the score was 2. A complete miss

TABLE XII.

Grading and Ranking on Motor Skill with the Cup and Ball.

	Average daily score for first 8 days. Right Hand.	Rank for Right Hand.	Percentage of inferiority of Left Hand.	Average daily score for second 8 days. Right Hand.	Rank for Right Hand.	Percentage of gain over first 8 days.	Percentage of inferiority of Left Hand.	Average daily score for last 9 days. Right Hand.	Rank for Right Hand.	Percentage of gain over first 8 days.	Percentage of inferiority of Left Hand.	Final Rank on score.	Final Rank on degree of inferiority of Left Hand.
A	24	14	−12.5	50	13	108	1.5	54	13	125	14.8	13	13
B	58	12	3.1	71	12	22.4	−9.6	86	9	48.2	9.3	12	14
C	62	10	9.7	74	10	19.3	10.8	75	10	20.9	12.	11	8
D	26	13	26.9	41	14	57.7	48.7	48	14	84.6	50.	14	1
E	59	11	15.3	75	9	27.1	6.6	88	8	49.1	11.3	10	7
F	78	3	6.4	99	1	27.	3.1	100	2	28.2	5.	2	12
G	68	7	5.8	76	8	11.7	1.3	62	12	−8.8	−30.6	8	11
H	93	1	22.5	95	3	2.	3.1	105	1	12.9	12.3	1	4
I	74	6	21.7	88	5	18.9	1.1	91	6	22.9	6.5	5	9
J	66	9	6.	84	7	27.2	9.5	89	7	34.8	20.2	7	6
K	76	4	17.1	98	2	28.9	18.3	100	2	31.5	17.	3	2
L	90	2	12.2	90	4	0	18.8	98	4	8.8	7.1	4	5
M	68	8	17.1	87	6	27.9	20.6	93	5	36.7	9.6	6	3
N	76	5	25.3	72	11	−4.	11.1	72	11	−4	−6.9	9	9

was scored 3. These numbers were then added together, the lowest score thus giving the best record. The results for each day were kept separate. Record was also kept of the number of times the ball not only missed but was swung far behind the cup at full length of the string. In the same way records were kept of the number of swings as much too short.

The preceding table gives the chief results according to a reverse method of computation. It will be seen that Group II are, on the whole, decidedly superior in this test. A and D rank so far below all the others as to form a group by themselves. Group II also show greater superiority of the right hand over the left than do Group I. F is left-handed but has been taught to write with right hand. The table gives but little idea of the extreme awkwardness of A and D.

2. *The arrow and trough.* A smooth wooden trough was constructed about 10 feet long and 1 inch wide. A light, smooth wooden arrow three feet long was then made, of a size to fit easily in the trough. The test was to lay the arrow in the trough so as to project an inch and then with a wooden paddle to strike the projecting end of the arrow and drive it to a given point. In these experiments the arrow was to be driven two feet. Trials to the number of 150 were given each subject, 50 a day for three succeeding visits, all with the right hand. The chief aim was to test muscle discrimination and motor memory.

Average deviation is the most important item in the result and the rank on it for the three sets of trials combined is:

GROUP I.

A	B	C	D	E	F	G
10	1	14	11	12	2	9

GROUP II.

H	I	J	K	L	M	N
3	4	7	12	5	6	8

B, F, and H show least variation in the average deviation for the three trials. A, C, E and M show most, and the others are between. There are also wide differences in practice gain. If we rank our subjects on this point we have:

GROUP I.

A	B	C	D	E	F	G
2	9	1	13	4	11	14

GROUP II.

H	I	J	K	L	M	N
12	7	9	5	6	3	8

The lack of correlation among the three separate trials indicates that the results on this test are not very reliable.

3. In order to learn the rate of motivation for some of the larger, more fundamental muscles the subjects were given three trials at running down stairs. A continuous series of six flights of ordinary stairs in the University building served for the purpose. This test was not very satisfactory for the reason that a good deal seemed to depend on how much risk of falling the subject was willing to take. I will give only the grade on a scale of three.

GROUP I.

A	B	C	D	E	F	G
1	1	1	3	3	3	3

GROUP II.

H	I	J	K	L	M	N
1	3	2	1	1	3	2

4. *Learning rhythmic movements.* The series of movements used was a variation of those accompanying the well known words "Bean porridge hot, bean porridge cold, bean porridge in the pot nine days old." It consists of slapping the hands in changing order, either together, on the knees, or against the hands of another person sitting opposite, who goes through the same movements. Some of the subjects had learned in the past series somewhat similar but so far unlike the one used that it is doubtful whether the results were affected.

Results. The subjects fall into three groups. 1. *B, C, F, G, H, J* and *N* perfected the series in 4 to 5 minutes. 2. *D* and *I* in 9 to 12 minutes. 3. *A, E, K, L* and *M* in 15 minutes and upward.

5. *Steadiness.* The subject was given a book and told to carry it about the room on his head. Though this would seem to be a very rough test, the results are interesting. All were able to perform the feat without great difficulty except three, *A, D,* and *I. I* could seldom get farther than 20 or 30 feet without letting the book fall, and *A* and *D* not over two or three steps, the book often falling off before they could get started. It will be remembered that *A* and *D* are the subjects so far inferior to the others with the cup and ball. There was also distinct difference in the nervous strain with which the feat was accomplished. Some of the subjects walked about with a smile, the arms relaxed, and step even and regular; others with firmly set jaws, the muscles of the neck tense, the head screwed awkwardly to one side, the arms held rigidly out from the body, the fingers cramped, and with stiff, jerky gait. *B, F, G, H, J* and *L* showed the least of this overflow of muscu-

lar innervation, A, D, and I most, while it was quite marked, though to a less degree, with C, E, K, M and N.

6. *Motor Automatisms.* For a discussion of the importance of motor automatisms as an index of nervous balance the reader is referred to Lindley's study of the motor phenomena of mental effort. (11.) Two of my subjects, C and D, were quite remarkable in this respect, keeping up continual and countless contortions of body and face, singing or whistling, twitching fingers, shuffling the feet, whispering, clucking, puffing out the cheeks, trilling the lips, corrugating the brows, fingering a pencil, tapping with fingers, getting up, turning on chair, etc. A, and to a less degree B, E, K and N, were also subject to automatisms. Relative to motor automatisms they may be graded on a scale of five, as follows:

GROUP I.

A	B	C	D	E	F	G
3	2	4	5	2	1	1

GROUP II.

H	I	J	K	L	M	N
1	1	1	2	1	1	2

A, C, and D are the striking cases. It will also be remembered that A and D were totally unable to walk with a book balanced on the head, and were ridiculously awkward with the cup and ball; nor could they shoot marbles. C is a stutterer and did rather poorly with cup and ball.

On the whole, then, the advantage in motor ability, in so far as it has been observed, lies with the stupid subjects, D and A being especially deficient. My results, therefore, so far as they show anything on the correlation of mental and motor skill would agree with those of Bagley in supporting a negative correlation.

XI. Individual Sketches. A. Age, 10 years 2 months. Weight, 63 lbs. Healthy and without marked physical defects. Of American parentage, son of a carpenter. Has attended school 5½ years and is in 6th grade. His teacher describes him as poor in drawing, but good in all his other work, being specially apt in arithmetic, and delighting in the solution of complicated problems. At school, also, he shows unusual inquisitiveness and desire for explanations. In the tests he takes rather low rank in invention, very high in mathematics, and extremely low in physical dexterity. His many automatisms are noted elsewhere. His awkwardness is well nigh indescribable. Several times he fell off his chair while going through his numerous contortions. Never acquired any dexterity with the cup and ball. In the latter exercise he was not only unable to get the cup in proper position for catching the ball, but never even learned to control the force of the swing. For two or three trials the ball was swung over his shoulder at full length of the string. Then would follow two or three attempts about as much too weak, the ball not rising enough to permit the cup to be placed under it. This same lack of motor control is seen in his inability to shoot marbles, to sing a simple tune, to learn to swim (though he tried almost every day during one summer), to learn complex movements with Indian clubs, or even to perform so apparently simple a feat as walking with a book balanced on the head. He is of lively and sunny disposition, but a little mischievous and even headstrong at times. His expression is lively, his eyes have a happy twinkle, and he often talks jocosely to himself as he works.

B. Age, 11 years 1 month. Weight, 76 lbs. Looks strong but has been ill a good deal. Hearing about ¼ normal, due to scarlet fever at the age of 7. A few months ago he underwent an operation for the removal of an adenoid. Father a successful business man of more than ordinary culture. Of American parentage and able to trace his ancestry back to an English earl of 250 years ago. Has attended school only 2½ years, and in the first of these years only about one-fourth of the time (by reason of illness). Regarded by teacher as possessing remarkable ability. She says his attention is wonderful, sometimes leading him to work until exhausted. The father also testified to the latter trait and related how when lying ill he propped himself up by pillows and covered the bed with books which were read as long as the physician allowed. Uniformly good in the mental tests. He is extremely neat, of fine bearing, cultured manners, and extraordinary command of spoken language. His experience has been broadened by travel and by acquaintance with numerous books. Has associated little with other children and has played few games. Expresses an ambition to graduate in college and university and to become a naturalist. May be described as logical and clear headed.

C. Age, 10 years 10 months. Weight, 73 lbs. Health good. Mild astigmatism and wears glasses. Of English and French descent and of fairly cultured family. In the 6th grade at school. Described by teacher as poor in spelling and arithmetic but talented in drawing and literature. Of flighty attention. This agrees with my own observations. He has quick perception but no will to work at what is not agreeable to his tastes. Of active, nervous temperament. Wants "to do things." Several times expressed dislike for mental tests and preference for the motor exercises. Slender, stutters badly, has many nervous automatisms. His teachers testify that his stuttering is much worse near the end of the school year. Has ambition to become an artist. Greatly interested also in literature and has read several novels. Once recounted to me the story of Dickens's Tale of two Cities. He told it in minute detail, and as he progressed became more and more excited, stuttered, talked rapidly, and showed great bodily agitation, standing up and then sitting down and all the time keeping up numerous automatisms. May be described as imaginative and poetical rather than logical.

D. Age, 10 years 5 months. Weight, 78 pounds. Tall and slender. Slight astigmatism and has worn glasses since he was four years old. Had an adenoid removed two years ago. Takes cold easily. Of cultured, middle-class family. In the 6th grade of school work. Gets his highest school grades in history and his lowest in numbers. Teacher notes the unusual facility with which he comprehends explanations, and his fine memory for all the school exercises. Ranks lower in the puzzles and chess than elsewhere. His attention is spontaneous and flitting. His work is done by brief strokes of attention. Often interrupts his work to talk of other things. Is quick to comprehend a witty remark, is vivacious, has very mobile facial expression. In the physical tests he ranks lowest of all. I have not observed such a lack of motor co-ordination in any other boy. He made little progress with the cup and ball, could not shoot marbles, was slow to learn rhythmic movements, often stumbled and fell, and like *A*, could not walk with book balanced on head. His automatic twitches extend almost to the point of chorea and his frown or smile shows bilateral asymmetry. He starts noticeably at all sudden or sharp sounds. He cannot carry an easy tune, and cannot write without making numerous blotches on his paper.

E. Age, 10 years 8 months. Weight, 55 lbs. Father a respectable Irish laborer. In good health, but undersized. In 5th grade at school. Gets lowest grades in arithmetic and highest in history and geography. In most of the mental tests he ranks below the others of group I, especially in mathematics and the puzzles. Does well with the fables. Is diffident, seldom speaks except when spoken to. Has large and expressive eyes. Is quick to catch explanations, but careless and inaccurate in all his work. Is slightly nervous and exhibits more automatisms than the subjects of group II. Employs rather childish expressions in the written exercises, seen especially in connecting together many sentences with "and." Rather intermittent attention.

F. 10 years 7 months old. Weight, 61 lbs. Father a respectable laborer. In good health. Has attended school 3½ years and is in the 5th grade. Gets "excellent" in all his school studies. His teacher testifies that he does not play boisterously at school like the other children and that during study hours he hardly looks off his books. When his lessons are done he reads. Ranks next to the lowest of group I in the puzzles. He is timid and reserved. Voice is hesitating. Facing a puzzle places his mind in a queer state self-consciousness and embarrassment. He says they make him "nervous." At such times his eyes assume a blank expression, and he seems distracted and unable to pull his thoughts together. The condition is a kind of *intellectual aboulia.* The flow of ideas seems to cease. Takes highest rank with cup and ball, is a swift runner and good at marbles. He is ambidextrous, throws with left hand but writes with the right.

G. Age, 11 years 5 months. Weight, 73½ lbs. Father a respectable Irish laborer, of more than average intelligence. Mother hysterical. Is a younger brother of *N*, but two years beyond him in school work. In school 6½ years and in eighth grade. Ranks uniformly high in all his school work as well as in all my mental tests. In latter is second only to *B*. Has had very narrow experience, never outside of the city of Worcester. Is not willing to leave his books long enough to help his mother with the chores, but leaves them for his brother, *N*, to do. Assumes a kind of guardianship over his older brother, *N*, when they visit my house together. Greatly interested in history and in current events. Logical and clear headed.

H. Age, 13 years 5 months. Weight, 84 lbs. Of a poor Swedish family of little culture. Hearing only ¾ normal. One eye astigmatic so as to be useless for reading. Only in the sixth grade and ranks uniformly low in all his school studies. Better than his group in invention and chess but very low in all the other mental tests. Has played checkers a great deal and his high rank in chess is probably due to this. Has read but three books and can tell little about these. Is good in the motor tests. Has done several kinds of work and plays baseball and football. Is a good swimmer. He is gruff, stolid, obtuse, apathetic, heavy. Very seldom laughs, talks little, and betrays few interests. Never begins a conversation with me and never talks confidentially. Says he will quit school this year and go to work.

7

I. Age, 10 years 4 months. Weight, 64 lbs. Father a respectable English laborer. Health good. Is in the 5th grade at school. Below medium in all his school work. Has read only two books. Uniformly poor in the mental tests. Shows a preference for the physical exercises. Is active, likes games and is apt at ball and marbles. He is neat in his person and work. He is quiet, reserved, talks little. Speech is hesitating and voice low. Little enthusiasm.

J. Age, 10 years 9 months. Weight, 109 lbs. Obese. Father a policeman of little culture. Irish descent. Health good, but he wears glasses to correct astigmatism. In the fifth grade at school. His teacher finds him extremely dull in all his work, untruthful, resentful, quarrelsome and incorrigible. On the playground he seldom joins with others in the games but prefers to lounge about with one or two companions. Very low in all the mental tests except invention. Fair motor ability. In his apathy much like *H.* Facial expression is stolid, blank, indifferent. Has only read three books. Was never out of the bounds of the city. While belonging to the same general type as *H,* is of decidedly higher grade of intelligence.

K. Age, 10 years 11 months. Weight, 62 lbs. Of an uncultured Swedish family. Health good, but teeth decayed. In 5th grade at school. Teacher gives him lowest rank in all his school work, says he is dreamy, fails to hear or to comprehend her directions, shows little curiosity, troubled or disturbed by nothing, lies, steals, cheats and has little sense of honor. My observations agree with the above. More than once his speech betrayed his low grade of moral concepts. At one time he related without any apparent shame how he "nearly beat the head off" his younger brother because the latter refused to deliver his newspapers for him. When asked if it was right to do that, he answered in the affirmative, on the ground that his brother should have obeyed him. High rank with the cup and ball but low in all the mental tests.

L. Age, 12 years 5 months. Weight, 78 lbs. Father an English laborer of little culture. No noticeable physical defects. In 6th grade at school. Does fairly good work in history and geography. Has read about a dozen books. In the puzzles and in use of language ranks far above his class. Often gave evidence of a certain shrewdness. Not emotional like *C* or *D* and yet not stolid like *H* or *J.* Plays many games well. Specially apt at ball and marbles. Has had much experience in caring for animals, as his father breeds dogs, goats, hares, ferrets, guinea pigs, birds, cocks, etc. He leads an outdoor life and is fairly observant. Not unusual in appearance and his reaction to the tests would lead one to expect from him better school work than his teacher finds.

M. Age, 11 years; weight, 68 lbs. Of well to do and cultured family. No noticeable physical defects. In 5th grade at school. Takes extremely low rank in all his studies, except that he takes pride in the neatness of his written work. Has read only three books and does not like to read. Does, however, like to be read to, and his mother has indulged him in this a great deal. In disposition he is quiet, unemotional, and seldom laughs. He plays games in a half-hearted way and has few close friends. He is an only child and prefers to be alone, often sitting quiet for hours with blank expression. Gets interested in certain simple games (usually such as require little physical movement) and busies himself at them for periods that would bore most children. Health seems good, but physical energy is apparently deficient. All his movements, whether mental or physical are slow. Exasperatingly slow to comprehend explanations. Goes about everything so deliberately as to make one wonder whether he has any perception of the passing of time. Neat in person and of good appearance.

N. Age, 13 years 9 months. Weight, 81 lbs. Hearing only ½ normal. Brother of *G.* In sixth grade, though he has attended school since the age of 4 years. His teacher finds him the most stupid pupil she ever had. Uniformly poor in all his studies. Never read a book. Says he can't get the meaning. Enjoys very much having his younger brother, *G,* read to him. *G* has read several books to him and *N* takes great interest in them. Normal, if not super-normal, memory for stories heard. His mother says he remembers better than *G.* In more than one respect *N*'s ability is puzzling. He is almost totally unable to read or spell and yet he has a fairly fluent command of spoken language. He also ranks outside his group in the ability to interpret fables. Greater age may contribute to this result but will not account for it in full. *H,* of nearly equal age, ranks 14 in the fable test. According to his teacher, *N* is stubborn, high tempered, easily offended, and childish in his play. My own observations confirm this. He realizes that he is duller than other children. The father, when trying to teach him, gets impatient and calls him a blockhead. At this the boy goes to another room and cries. Interests extensive enough, but shallow and lacking permanence. He stands in interesting contrast with *H* or *M.* The latter belong to Kraepelin's dull type of sub-normal mentality, while *N* is a good example of the lively type. He has good facial expression and is handsome. In movements he is rather awkward. He is a confirmed bed-wetter.

XII. SUMMARY AND REMARKS.

1. The following table represents the ranking of each subject in each group of tests.

TABLE XIII.

Ranking on All Tests.

	Invention.	Logical processes.	Mathematical ability.	Language.	Interpretation of Fables.	Chess.	Memory.	Cup and Ball motor test.
A	10	5	1	6	8	7	6	13
B	1	1	1	1	1	1	3	12
C	4	3	4	3	2	2	2	11
D	3	6	5	4	6	8	4	14
E	9	8	7	8	4	6	10	10
F	7	4	6	4	6	5	5	1
G	2	2	3	2	3	3	1	8
H	5	10	10	14	14	4	14	2
I¡	11	12	12	10	9	11	13	5
J	7	13	11	9	12	10	11	7
K	13	14	12	12	10	13	9	3
L	5	7	8	6	13	9	6	4
M	14	11	14	13	10	14	11	6
N	11	9	9	10	5	12	8	9

2. Group I is superior to group II in all the mental tests, and inferior in the motor tests.

3. The superiority of group I is about the same for all the mental tests except those coming under the head of invention, where it is less.

4. On the whole, the standing of the individual subjects through the separate tests is strikingly uniform. This is only another way of saying that intelligence in these subjects does not show a decided tendency to develop along special lines.

5. Group II discloses no inferiority to group I in the amount of persistency with which problems are attacked. On the contrary, *H*, *J*, and *M* are among the most persistent workers, while *A*, *C*, *D* and *E* show more fitfulness and spurtiness. The latter, to be sure, usually accomplish more in a short period of time than the former in a longer, but their attention is more easily distracted. They more often interrupt a solution to talk of foreign matters, or to engage in some other unrelated activity. The respective methods of work indicate on the part of the latter mental associations that are more volatile, more spontaneous, and based on more subtle resemblances; on the part of the former, associations that are close, matter of fact, and labored.

6. All the subjects were asked (individually of course) whether they preferred to read or to play games. With the exception of *E*, who gave an uncertain answer, all of group I replied that they preferred reading. Every subject of group II preferred games. It would be interesting to know how much a certain innate aversion to physical exercise, or even a lack of encouragement of the same, due to pecularities of the environment, might contribute to the building up or even the creation of interests in such affairs as school work and books. The reverse possibility is also worthy of investigation.

7. Indications of emotional differences, noted elsewhere, are striking and are no doubt closely bound up with the observed intellectual differences.

8. While offering little positive data on the subject, the study has strengthened my impression of the relatively greater importance of *endowment* over *training*, as a determinant of an individual's intellectual rank among his fellows.

In closing, I take pleasure in expressing my great obligations to Dr. E. C. Sanford, not only for assistance throughout the study but also for careful criticism of the entire manuscript To President G. Stanley Hall, and Dr. W. H. Burnham, I am indebted for frequent counsel and advice; to Dr. Fred Kuhlmann for able assistance in the tests, and to him, as well as to Dr. G. E. Partridge, for many suggestions in planning the study and in treatment of the data. For other valuable assistance and for their friendly interest in the work I wish to thank Dr. Theodate L. Smith, Dr. Louis N. Wilson, Dr. W. F. Book, and Dr. A. L. Gesell.

REFERENCES.

1. BAIN, A. On the study of character. Parker, London, 1861. pp. 334.
2. BOLTON, T. L. The relation of motor power to intelligence. *Am. Jour. of Psy.*, July, Oct., 1903, Vol. 14, pp. 351-367.
3. BRVAN, W. L. Theory and practice. Psy. Rev., 1904, N. S., Vol. 11, pp. 71-82.
4. CATTELL, J. McK. Examinations, grades and credits. Pop. Sci. Mo., 1904-1905, Vol. 66, pp. 367-378.
5. EBBINGHAUS, H. Ueber eine neue methode zur Prufung geistige Fähigkeiten und ihre Anwendung bei Schulkindern. Zeits. fur Psy. u. Physiol. der Sinnesorgane, 1896, Vol. 13, pp. 401-457.
6. GESELL, A. L. Accuracy in handwriting, as related to school intelligence and sex. *Am. Jour. of Psy.*, July, 1905, Vol. 17, pp. 344-405.
7. HODGE, C. F. Method of homing pigeons. Pop. Sci. Mo., 1894, Vol. 44, pp. 758-775.
8. JAMES, W. Psychology; briefer course. See preface. Holt, New York, 1904. pp. 478.
9. KINNAMAN, A. J. The mental life of two macacus rhesus monkeys in captivity. *Am. Jour. of Psy.*, Jan., 1902, Vol. 13, pp. 98-148.
10. KIRKPATRICK, E. A. Individual tests of school children. Psy. Rev., May, 1900. Vol. 7, pp. 274-280.
11. LINDLEY, E. H. Preliminary study of some of the motor phenomena of mental effort. *Am. Jour. of Psy.*, July, 1896, Vol. 7, pp. 491-517.
12. —— —— Psychology of puzzles, with special reference to the psychology of mental adaptation. *Am. Jour. of Psy.*, July, 1897, Vol. 8, pp. 431-493.
13. MACH, E. On the part played by accident in invention and discovery. Monist, Jan., 1896, Vol. 6, pp. 161-175.
14. MASON, O. T. Origins of invention. Scott, London, 1902. pp. 419.
15. MEZES, S. E. Essentials of human faculty. Univ. of Cal., Publications.
16. PAULHAN, F. Psychologie de l'invention. Alcan, Paris, 1901. pp. 184.
17. SIMON, —— Experiences de copie. L'Année Psy., 1900, Vol. 7, pp. 490-518.
18. SPEARMAN C. General intelligence objectively determined and measured. *Am. Jour. of Psy.*, Apr., 1904, Vol. 15, pp. 201-293.
19. STERN, L. W. Ueber Psychologie der individuellen Differenzen. Barth, Leipzig, 1900. pp. 146.
20. SWIFT, E. J. Standards of efficiency in school and in life. Ped. Sem., Mch., 1903, Vol. 10, pp. 3-22.
21. THORNDIKE, E. L. Educational psychology. Lemcke, New York, 1903. pp. 177.
22. TITCHENER, E. B. The problems of experimental psychology. *Am. Jour. of Psy.*, Apr., 1905, Vol. 16, pp. 208-224.
23. WILLIAMS, H. S. What is research? Pop. Sci. Mo., 1905, Vol. 67, pp. 170-177.

Classics In
Child Development

An Arno Press Collection

Baldwin, James Mark. **Thought and Things.** Four vols. in two. 1906-1915

Blatz, W[illiam] E[met], et al. **Collected Studies on the Dionne Quintuplets.** 1937

Bühler, Charlotte. **The First Year of Life.** 1930

Bühler, Karl. **The Mental Development of the Child.** 1930

Claparède, Ed[ouard]. **Experimental Pedagogy and the Psychology of the Child.** 1911

Factors Determining Intellectual Attainment. 1975

First Notes by Observant Parents. 1975

Freud, Anna. **Introduction to the Technic of Child Analysis.** 1928

Gesell, Arnold, et al. **Biographies of Child Development.** 1939

Goodenough, Florence L. **Measurement of Intelligence By Drawings.** 1926

Griffiths, Ruth. **A Study of Imagination in Early Childhood and Its Function in Mental Development.** 1918

Hall, G. Stanley and Some of His Pupils. **Aspects of Child Life and Education.** 1907

Hartshorne, Hugh and Mark May. **Studies in the Nature of Character. Vol. I: Studies in Deceit; Book One, General Methods and Results.** 1928

Hogan, Louise E. **A Study of a Child.** 1898

Hollingworth, Leta S. **Children Above 180 IQ, Stanford Binet:** Origins and Development. 1942

Kluver, Heinrich. **An Experimental Study of the Eidetic Type.** 1926

Lamson, Mary Swift. **Life and Education of Laura Dewey Bridgman, the Deaf, Dumb and Blind Girl.** 1881

Lewis, M[orris] M[ichael]. **Infant Speech:** A Study of the Beginnings of Language. 1936

McGraw, Myrtle B. **Growth: A Study of Johnny and Jimmy.** 1935

Monographs on Infancy. 1975

O'Shea, M. V., editor. **The Child: His Nature and His Needs.** 1925

Perez, Bernard. **The First Three Years of Childhood.** 1888

Romanes, George John. **Mental Evolution in Man:** Origin of Human Faculty. 1889

Shinn, Milicent Washburn. **The Biography of a Baby.** 1900

Stern, William. **Psychology of Early Childhood Up to the Sixth Year of Age.** 1924

Studies of Play. 1975

Terman, Lewis M. **Genius and Stupidity:** A Study of Some of the Intellectual Processes of Seven "Bright" and Seven "Stupid" Boys. 1906

Terman, Lewis M. **The Measurement of Intelligence.** 1916

Thorndike, Edward Lee. **Notes on Child Study.** 1901

Wilson, Louis N., compiler. **Bibliography of Child Study.** 1898-1912

[Witte, Karl Heinrich Gottfried]. **The Education of Karl Witte,** Or the Training of the Child. 1914